AQA Psychology A

A2

Psychology

Research Methods Workbook

D0928989

Julia Willerton
Dominic Helliwell
Nick Lund

Nelson Thornes

00290

Published in 2011 by:
Nelson Thornes Ltd
Delta Place
27 Bath Road
CHELTENHAM
GL53 7TH
United Kingdom

11 12 13 14 15 / 10 9 8 7 6 5 4 3 2 1

A catalogue record for this book is available from the British Library

ISBN 978 1 4085 0818 3

Cover photograph: Evan Sharboneau/iStockphoto

Page make-up by Pantek Arts Ltd, Maidstone

Printed and bound in Spain by GraphyCems

Contents

This workbook is designed to help you broaden your understanding of psychological research by carrying out actual psychological research yourself. You will also develop your critical understanding by thinking and talking with your teachers and fellow students. Discuss what worked well – but remember that you can learn as much, if not more, when things do not go as planned and a null hypothesis is retained. Carrying out practical work will also help you to write more effectively when answering exam questions about the strengths and weaknesses of particular research methods.

The research projects in this book are related to the different topics in psychology that you will be studying at A2 and will help you to tackle the research methods section of the PSYA4 examination. You can memorise methodological concepts from a textbook, but putting them to use in practical work will really help you to understand them.

Each research project includes:

Learning outcomes

The learning objectives for all of the practicals are listed below. Check the start of each practical to see which learning objectives it covers.

A   Making design decisions
A1 Select an appropriate research method (experimental or non-experimental)
A2 Select appropriate investigation design and/or research techniques and tools
A3 Identify and operationalise variables
A4 Identify and control extraneous variables
A5 Understand the importance of ethics

B   Implementing design decisions
B1 Practise writing null and experimental hypotheses
B2 Design and construct apparatus/materials
B3 Design standardised instructions
B4 Understand how to select samples

C   Collecting and recording data
C1 Understand how to ask for consent and debrief participants afterwards
C2 Collect qualitative data in the form of written responses
C3 Collect quantitative data
C4 Carry out a content analysis
C5 Convert qualitative data into quantitative form for statistical analysis

D   Displaying data and descriptive statistics
D1 Summarise findings of your study using descriptive statistics
D2 Display data using appropriate graphical techniques
D3 Display descriptive statistics

E   Analysing and interpreting data
E1 Carry out a test of association (chi-square)
E2 Carry out a test of correlation (Spearman's rho)
E3 Carry out a test of difference (Mann-Whitney U test)
E4 Carry out a test of difference (Wilcoxon)
E5 Interpret the results in terms of statistical significance

Background

There is a brief summary of the theoretical background to the topic. The Key study is a quick reminder of a related study.

Method

Each practical includes step-by-step instructions to carry out the research.

Think about

These features highlight particular aspects that are important to consider when carrying out research or answering questions on research methods in your exam.

Critical discussion

This includes some of the more important points that you may want to consider and discuss after you have collected and analysed your data.

Glossary and Appendix

Terms relating to research methods can be found in the glossary, and the Appendix contains key documents, including statistical tables.

Ethical issues

Carrying out these research projects will help you to develop your understanding of research within an ethical framework. Ethical issues are raised throughout, but this does not mean that all of the ethical issues have been thought out for you. Whenever you carry out research involving feeling, thinking beings, including both human and non-human animals, you need to be aware of possible ethical issues at all stages of the research process. For this reason, the BPS ethical guidelines are included in the Appendix.

Reporting psychological investigations

There are conventions for reporting psychological research. The table below shows the different sections that are generally needed in a report.

Table 1 *Report sections*

Section	Function
Title	To tell the reader what the report is about
Abstract	To provide the reader with a brief summary of the study
Introduction	To introduce the background and rationale of the study
Method	To describe how the study was done
Results	To summarise the findings
Discussion	To discuss the findings and their implications
References	To inform the reader about the sources of information
Appendices	Can be used for detailed information not in the report

Biological rhythms and sleep

1 Alertness and time of day

> **Learning outcomes for this practical**
> - A1, A2, A3, A4, A5, B1, B3, B4, C1, C3, D3, E4, E5

Hint

Check these learning outcomes against the list on page iv.

Background

Biological rhythms are found in most living organisms. There are a number of biological rhythms that affect human beings. Some of these are ultradian rhythms that occur in a period of less than one day (e.g. every 90 minutes). Other rhythms are infradian and these occur over a period of more than one day (e.g. every month or year). Many of the rhythms studied by psychologists tend to be circadian rhythms. These are rhythms that occur over an approximate 24-hour or daily period. Research suggests that there may be over a hundred such rhythms that affect human physiological and psychological processes. For example, temperature and a variety of hormones and neurotransmitters fluctuate in a circadian rhythm. The most obvious behavioural circadian rhythm is the sleep–wake cycle. Psychological factors affected by circadian rhythms include STM, executive function (decision making) and sensitivity to pain. (Research suggests we are least sensitive to head and face pain at 2pm, so this may be the best time to make dentist appointments!)

Look it up …

Refresh your memory about biological rhythms by looking at your A2 Student Book.

One psychological variable that has been studied is alertness. Our level of alertness affects our ability to perform actions efficiently and therefore has important consequences for things such as safety at work or driving ability. One of the first to report this was Blake (1967). Blake measured participants' performance on a range of tasks (including card sorting and visual search) at various points of the day from early morning to the evening. The tasks were used as a measure of alertness. The participants performed the tasks best at 10.30am and worst at 2pm. The lowering of alertness in the early afternoon has been called the post-lunch dip (Monk, 2005).

Think about controls

How could you check to see whether the post-lunch dip was the result of time of day or of eating food at lunchtime?

The effect of time of day on the level of alertness has been studied in a variety of ways both in the laboratory and in real life. One method of assessing the level of alertness in laboratory studies is to measure variables that are linked to alertness, such as reaction time. These tend to give precise measures, but they do not take into account how participants feel. Other researchers have devised self-report scales that allow participants to report on their subjective assessment of their alertness level. Real-life studies include studies of performance of clerical tasks in offices or analyses of traffic accidents. Both the laboratory and real-life studies suggest there is a post-lunch dip in alertness. This practical exercise involves testing alertness at different times of the day.

Method

Step 1 *Design your study: variables and hypotheses*

The first step of the research process is to identify a topic of interest and to choose a suitable method to investigate it. Here, the topic of interest is the difference in alertness of participants at different times of the day and the method will be a natural experiment.

In a natural experiment, the researcher does not manipulate an independent variable directly but measures the effect of a naturally occurring independent variable upon a dependent variable. The independent variable and the dependent variable in this natural experiment are as follows:

- independent variable: the time of day
- dependent variable: the level of alertness.

As any measures of levels of alertness vary greatly between participants, it would be difficult to compare different groups of people at different times of the day. In other words, an independent group design is not ideal for this study as the group chosen for the pre-lunch test may be generally more alert than the post-lunch group. An alternative, which is a better choice in this case, is to use a repeated measure design where the alertness of one group of participants is tested pre- and post-lunch. However, there are disadvantages to using this method as well, and you will need to consider these in your critical discussion.

Explain one disadvantage of using the repeated measure design for this study.

_____

_____

An important aspect of this study is to operationalise the variables. The independent and dependent variable as stated above are not operationalised and are vague. You will need to choose two times of the day to use for the independent variable. The ideal times would be 10.30am and 2pm as research has shown that these represent peaks and troughs, though this may not be practical for your timetable. The dependent variable is the level of alertness, but you need to decide how it is to be measured. There are two types of measure that can be used: self-report scales or measures of performance. Consider the advantages and disadvantages of both.

Think about validity

If a researcher did choose an independent group design, would it affect internal or external validity?

Think about controls

Remember that participants eating lunch is an extraneous variable and possibly a confounding variable. How would you address this issue?

Ethical issues

Remember to include any ethical advantages and problems of using a particular method if appropriate.

Measure	Advantages	Problems
Self-report scales		
Performance (e.g. reaction time)		

For this study it is easiest to use a simple measure of reaction time as an indication of levels of alertness.

Write the hypotheses for your study. The null hypothesis states that there will be no difference between condition X and Y, whereas the experimental hypothesis predicts a difference between the conditions. You will need to decide whether your experimental hypothesis should be directional (it uses a one-tailed test) or non-directional (it uses a two-tailed test). Non-directional hypotheses are chosen when there is insufficient research to point to the outcome of the study.

Write your hypotheses here.

■ *Null hypothesis* _____

■ *Alternative (experimental) hypothesis* _____

Justify your choice of a directional or non-directional hypothesis here:

I have chosen a _____ *hypothesis because* _____

_____

Step 2 *Sampling*

In this study, you will need to examine a group of participants at two different times of the day, before lunch and after lunch. In choosing your sample, you will have to consider the availability of the participants at the different times and how to study them.

There are a few different ways to select the participants:

■ a random sample

■ an opportunity sample

■ a self-selected (volunteer) sample.

You will also have to think about sample size.

Chosen sample method: _____

Look it up …

Refresh your memory in relation to the different methods of sampling by looking back at these in your A2 Student Book and thinking about the advantages and disadvantages of each of them.

Step 3 *Create materials and data sheets*

A simple but effective means of measuring reaction time is to record how quickly a participant can catch a 30 cm ruler. It requires one experimenter to test each participant. The experimenter should hold the ruler vertically and position it between the thumb and index finger of the preferred hand of the participant. The participant's arm should rest on a flat surface to prevent him or her moving the hand up or down. The participant should not touch the ruler, and the 0 cm mark should be level with the finger and thumb. Then, without any signal, the experimenter should release the ruler. The participant's task is to catch the ruler as quickly as he or she can. The level in centimetres just above the participant's finger is recorded. This should be repeated three times to get an average score in centimetres. The scores, in centimetres, give an indication of the time it takes to react to the ruler dropping.

Devise a set of standardised instructions for your participants that make it clear exactly what they need to do.

Create a simple sheet to record your data. This should show the average reaction time for each participant at the two different times of day.

Step 4 Ethical issues

Ethical issues guide practical choices and decisions at all stages of the research process. Think about the ethical issues involved in this piece of research.

- An important principle of research is to enable participants to give their fully informed consent to take part, knowing what they will be letting themselves in for. Tell potential participants what is involved in the study, what they will be asked to do and roughly how long it will take. You should let them know that you would like to study their reaction times in the morning and again in the afternoon. Put this information with a consent form and present it to the participants to sign. You can view a sample consent form in the Appendix. The consent form should make it clear to your participants that they are free to withdraw at any time.

- Ensure that your research does not put your participants under stress or make them feel uncomfortable. You may find that some participants do not want their performance to be public. Be sensitive to this when collecting your data. Participants should have the right to keep their data confidential and this extends to the collection as well as the storage of data.

- Ensure participants are fully debriefed at the end of the study. You should thank the participants, tell them what you expect to find and ask whether they have any questions. This is good ethical practise. You should remember to thank every participant after they have taken part.

Step 5 Piloting

A pilot study is the last stage of planning, before real data are collected. It enables you to check that your instructions and procedure work smoothly. Think about how and where you will collect your data. The location should be relatively noise- and distraction-free. Remember that this is a repeated measure design and that the environment you use should be kept the same (as far as is practically possible) for all of the participants in both conditions.

Carry out a short pilot study testing three or four people to check that your instructions and procedure work smoothly.

> **Think about controls**
>
> As well as ensuring the environment is kept the same, remember to standardise the time since participants ate lunch and the wait period between positioning the ruler and releasing it.

Record any problems or changes that need to be made to your instructions/procedure here.

_____

_____

Analysing your data

Step 6 *Organise and display your data*

You should have a completed data sheet with two average scores for each participant, one for the morning and the other for the afternoon condition. Such a mass of data can be very confusing to someone reading a report about your experiment, so the first stage of analysis is to organise your data and display it clearly.

The first stage in this is to present a measure of central tendency and a measure of dispersion for both conditions. The measures shown below are the median and the range.

	Median score (cm)	Range (cm)
Morning condition		
Afternoon condition		

Any differences in median scores could be shown effectively in a bar chart. What difference, if any, does the bar chart show for your data?

_____

_____

_____

_____

Step 7 *Inferential statistics and testing for significance*

In order to test for significance, psychologists carry out statistical tests, which show the likelihood that the difference obtained is real (significant) rather than occurring purely by chance. Your statistical test is chosen using a number of types of information:

- What level of data was collected – nominal or ordinal?
- Did the research look for a difference between sets of data or a relationship between two variables?
- If an experiment has been carried out, what type of design was used?

Write down the statistical test you will use.

_____

Look it up ...

You can refresh your memory about measures of central tendency and dispersion by looking at your A2 Student Book.

Think about it

Usually with interval data such as centimetres, the mean would be the appropriate measure of central tendency, but the centimetres here only give an indication of the time taken to react to the ruler dropping. This means that the data become ordinal and so the median is a more appropriate measure.

Look it up ...

You can refresh your memory about test choice using the flow chart in the Appendix (page 91).

Put your data into a table like the one below.

Participant	Morning condition	Afternoon condition	Difference	Rank order
1				
2				
3				
4				
5				
6				
7				
8				

- Calculate the difference between the scores in each condition. It is important to record the direction of difference (i.e. whether it is a positive or negative difference).
- Rank the differences ignoring whether they are positive or negative. Zero differences are disregarded and are not given a rank.
- Sum the ranks of the positive differences.
- Find the sum of the ranks of the negative differences.

The smallest of these is T, the notation for the Wilcoxon statistic.

This final number is your observed value of Wilcoxon. Write it here.

_____

Step 8 *Interpret your results. Is the result statistically significant?*

Assess whether the relationship you have found is statistically significant or could have occurred by chance. Compare your observed value with the critical value taken from the table in the Appendix. In order to find the critical value, you will need to use the following information:

- Decide where to look in the table by finding N, which is the number of pairs of scores that have been ranked. This may not be all of the pairs in the sample, as pairs that have a zero difference are not ranked.
- Check whether you had a directional or non-directional hypothesis.
- Find the column for probability level of 0.05 for either one- or two-tailed.
- The figure at the point in the table where these intersect is known as the critical value.

- If the observed value is equal to or less than the critical value, you can reject the null hypothesis and accept the alternative hypothesis that there was a difference between the morning and afternoon condition.

- If the observed value is greater than the critical value, you must retain the null hypothesis. Your data suggest that there is no difference in alertness at different times of the day.

- Complete the statistical conclusion below.

> The observed value of **T** = _____
>
> This was _____ than the critical value of _____
>
> for **N** = _____ probability equal to 0.05
>
> Therefore the null hypothesis was _____

Critical discussion

Theory

- Did your findings support the previous evidence that there is a post-lunch dip in alertness?
- If you retained the null hypothesis, can you think of reasons why this might be?
- Are there other variables that might account for your findings? (For example, individual differences and the idea that some people are morning types and others are evening types, or different chronotypes).

Methodology

- Did you have an appropriate number of participants?
- Were there problems using the repeated measure design?
- Was your measure of reaction time accurate?
- Does this measure provide a valid measure of alertness?
- Were your standardised instructions clear?

Ethics

- Did your study throw up any unseen ethical issues?
- How did your participants feel about taking part?
- What have you learned about research with people?

> **Think about validity**
>
> You probably had to use an opportunity sample for this study. How does this type of sample affect validity?

References

Blake, M.J.F. (1967) Time of day effects on performance in a range of tasks. *Psychonomic Science*, **9**, 349–50.

Monk, T.H. (2005) The post-lunch dip in performance. *Clinical Sports Medicine*, **24**, e15–e23.

Perception

2 | Investigating a visual illusion

Learning outcomes for this practical

- A1, A2, A4, A5, B1, B2, B3, B4, C1, C3, D1, E3, E5

Hint

Check these learning outcomes against the list on page iv.

Background

When we are presented with a visual illusion, there are certain factors that make it likely we will interpret what we see in a particular way. These factors include things like previous experience, expectation, context, motivation, beliefs and values. They are collectively referred to as 'perceptual set', as they predispose us to see something in a particular way. Perceptual set forms an important part of the study of perceptual organisation.

One of the oldest and best-known visual illusions is the Müller-Lyer illusion. In its traditional format the visual illusion comprises two horizontal lines of exactly the same length, each with angled fins on the ends. On one line the fins are angled inwards and on the other line they are angled outwards. Participants are asked whether they think the horizontal lines are the same length, or whether one is longer than the other. Most people will judge the line with the fins pointing outwards as being longer.

There have been various hypotheses to explain why this illusion occurs. Segall *et al.* (1963) focused on the 'impact of cultural experiences' and investigated these using cross-cultural studies. This gave rise to the carpentered world hypothesis, which suggests that we automatically apply our knowledge about buildings and perspective to interpret the Müller-Lyer illusion:

- The line with the fins pointing outwards looks like the inside corner of a building, where two walls meet.
- The other line (with the fins pointing inwards) looks like the outside corner of a building where two walls meet.

We automatically interpret this information using size constancy. Size constancy is developed along with other kinds of constancy when we are infants. It relates to the understanding that distant objects create a smaller retinal image, but are actually the same size. A simple example of this is the way in which real cars, viewed from a tall building, appear like toy cars. Applying this automatic knowledge, we assume that the corner with the fins pointing outwards is further away, and therefore we judge it to be larger. Thus we are fooled by the Müller-Lyer illusion.

The argument for the carpentered world hypothesis has been challenged and developed by research such as Howe and Purves (2004), who argued that there are many cues in the natural world that help us to interpret such figures. They point to several examples of images in nature that have similarities to the angles of the Müller-Lyer illusion. This means that even people who do not live in a carpentered environment will have had experiences that make them susceptible to this illusion.

Research has been undertaken specifically to investigate the influence that the fin angles have on the strength of the effect of the Müller-Lyer illusion (e.g. Dewar (1967); Restle and Decker (1977)). It has been shown that different fin angles create different amounts of distortion. This practical is designed to test whether people are deceived more by fins of one angle than another. You will construct a version of the illusion with fins at 45° to the horizontal and a version with fins at a 60° angle. This will assist you in drawing conclusions regarding the above argument.

> **Think about it**
>
> The lower the fin angle the greater the effect of this illusion, as the lower fin angle makes the arrow head appear more 'pointy'. We would expect a fin angle of 45° to lead to a greater error than a fin angle of 60°. This informs the choice of a directional hypothesis or a non-directional hypothesis.

The Müller-Lyer illusion

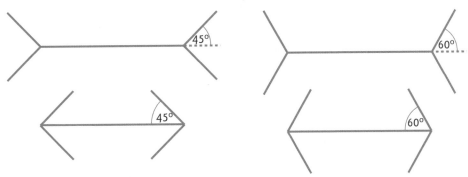

Method

Step 1 *Create your apparatus*

Take two pieces of A4 card and draw the lines shown in the diagram below. There are three things you must consider when doing this:

1 Point *B* must be right at the edge of the card.
2 The line *AB* must be shorter than the horizontal line on the second piece of card.
3 The fins should all be the same length and the same angle: 45°.

Repeat steps 1 to 3 on two new pieces of card, but this time draw the fins at an angle of 60° from the horizontal. How the cards are used and how your apparatus should look are shown here.

> **Look it up ...**
>
> There have been many cross-cultural studies investigating the impact of experience on perception. Read some of them and determine whether they all drew the same conclusions, that different experiences lead to different perceptions.

The two pieces of card

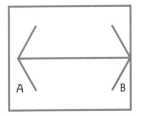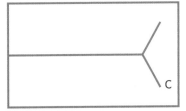

One card is placed over the other as shown and pulled apart until the lines seem to be the same length

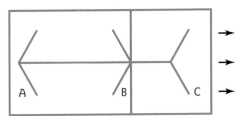

Step 2 *Design your study: variables and hypotheses*

This study investigates whether fin angle has an impact on how accurately someone is able to compare the two horizontal lines of the Müller-Lyer illusion.

As this is an experiment, you will need to identify the independent variable and the dependent variable:

- The independent variable is the angle of the fins (45° or 60°).
- The dependent variable is the average error made when comparing the two lines in each condition.

Your dependent variable needs to be measured in centimetres to the nearest millimetre.

Write the hypotheses for your study. The null hypothesis states that the independent variable will have no effect on the dependent variable, whereas the experimental hypothesis predicts that there will be an effect. You will need to decide whether your experimental hypothesis should be directional (use a one-tailed test) or non-directional (use a two-tailed test). Non-directional hypotheses are chosen when there is insufficient research to point to the outcome of the study or when previous research studies have produced conflicting results (i.e. you do not know what the outcome will be).

> *Write your hypotheses here.*
>
> - *Null hypothesis* _____
>
> - *Alternative (experimental) hypothesis* _____
>
> *Justify your choice of a directional or non-directional hypothesis here:*
>
> *I have chosen a* _____ *hypothesis because* _____
>
> _____

Think about it

You could conduct this experiment using a repeated measures design – letting each participant view both sets of lines. This would remove participant variables. However, it would create the possibility of order effects, so you would need to counterbalance the procedure by showing half of the participants the 45° fins first, and the other half the 60° fins first.

Think about it

With an independent groups design, the Mann-Whitney U test is used, but if you used a repeated measures design, it would mean having to use the Wilcoxon signed ranks test instead.

Step 3 *The procedure*

- Measure the length of the lines you have drawn from point *A* to point *B* in both conditions. (It would be ideal if these two lines were the same length.) Now you know what the correct answer should be.
- For each condition, place the second card underneath the *AB* line, sticking out far enough for point *C* to be visible, with the two horizontal lines meeting at point *B*.
- Construct a set of standardised instructions to read to each participant.
- Include asking each participant to pull out the second card until they think the distance from *B* to *C* is the same as the distance from *A* to *B*.
- When they have done this, measure the distance from point *B* to point *C*.
- Repeat this process with the second set of cards so that you have a figure for the lines with the 45° fin angle and one for the 60° fin angle.

- Whatever the distances are, subtract the actual lengths of *AB* and you will find the participant's error.
- Write each error in a table ready to perform your statistical analysis.
- You can tell the participants what their errors were if they want to know. Ensure that they understand this is a measure of the effectiveness of an optical illusion, not a test of their abilities. This should form part of your debriefing process.

Think about it

Participant variables are an extraneous, and potentially confounding, variable. This needs to be addressed by random allocation of participants to the two conditions.

Step 4 *Sampling*

In this study you will need two groups of participants belonging to one of two conditions. Group one will be asked to judge the length of the lines with a 45° fin angle, and group two will be asked to judge the length of the lines with a 60° fin angle. There are a few different ways to select your participants:

- random sampling
- opportunity sampling
- self-selecting (volunteer) sampling.

You have to decide whether to use a very simple method to obtain participants or, if you think participant variables might be an issue, whether to ensure the sample is representative by using a more complicated method. Also you should decide how many people are required. You need enough participants to increase the chances of your results being statistically significant, but not so many that your calculations become difficult. (An alternative method would be to use a repeated measures design as outlined in the Think about it at the top of page 10.)

Hint

Remember that when you analyse your results, the limitations of both the sample and the sampling method should be considered in your conclusion.

Step 5 *Ethical issues*

Ethical issues guide practical choices and decisions at all stages of the research process. Think about the ethical issues involved in this piece of research.

- An important principle of research is to enable participants to give their fully informed consent to take part, knowing what they will be letting themselves in for. Tell potential participants what is involved in the study, what they will be asked to do and roughly how long it will take. Put this information onto a consent form and ask the participants to sign it. You can view a sample consent form in the Appendix on page 92. The consent form should make it clear to the participants that they are free to withdraw at any time.
- Ensure that your research does not put your participants under stress or make them feel uncomfortable. If people have poor eyesight, they might be reluctant to undergo a perception test. You need to be aware of this.
- Ensure participants are fully debriefed at the end of the study. Tell them what you expect to find and ask whether they have any questions. This is good ethical practice. Remember to thank all of the participants after they have taken part.

Step 6 *Piloting*

A pilot study is the last stage of planning, before real data are collected. It enables you to check that your materials, instructions and procedures work smoothly. Think about how and where you will collect your data. The environment you use should be kept the same (as far as is practically possible) for all of the participants, so it can be ruled out as a variable. The location should be relatively noise- and distraction-free (e.g. no mobile phones interrupting the procedure). Test people without others around to influence them. Make sure that the participants understand what they are supposed to do, and that you can measure the line accurately. One variable to consider in this study is eyesight. This is something to think about with your sample. Do you have a high number of participants who wear glasses? If so, then their eyesight or the potentially distorting effect of the lenses might have an impact on the answers they provide.

Carry out a short pilot study testing three or four people to check that your materials and procedures work smoothly.

> **Think about it**
> Aim to be consistent in relation to where, when and how your data are collected. Why do you think it is important to test people without their friends around?

Record any problems or changes needed to your procedures/instructions here.

_____

_____

Analysing your data

Step 7 *Organise and display your data*

You should have a completed data sheet with the error measured in centimetres for each participant, in two columns. One column is for the participants shown the 45° fins and one is for the participants shown the 60° fins. You should also calculate the mean for each group. The table below also includes the ranks of each score, and this is explained in step 8.

Put your data into a table like the example below.

Group A (45° fins)			Group B (60° fins)		
Participants	Error in cm	Rank	Participants	Error in cm	Rank
1	1.4	4	9	2.6	10
2	3	12.5	10	1.1	2
3	2.3	7.5	11	1.7	5
4	2.7	11	12	2.4	9
5	4.1	16	13	0.8	1
6	3.5	15	14	3.3	14
7	1.2	3	15	3	12.5
8	2.2	6	16	2.3	7.5
Mean	2.55		**Mean**	2.15	
Ra		75	**Rb**		61

You should also put the data into a bar chart like the one below. Do not include individual scores as this only presents participant differences. You need one bar for each condition – use the mean for each group. Make sure that the bar chart is fully labelled and headed, referring to both the independent and the dependent variables.

Bar chart of results

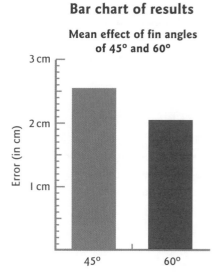

Mean effect of fin angles of 45° and 60°

Step 8 *Inferential statistics and testing for significance*

In order to test for significance, psychologists carry out statistical tests to show the likelihood that the relationship/difference obtained is real (significant) rather than occurring purely by chance. You will choose your statistical test using a number of types of information:

- What level of data was collected – nominal or ordinal?
- Did the research look for a difference between sets of data or a relationship between two variables?
- If an experiment has been carried out, what type of design was used?

> *Write down the statistical test you will use.*
>
> _____

Look it up …

You can refresh your memory about test choice using the flow chart in the Appendix on page 91.

If you have answered the three questions above correctly, you will have arrived at the Mann-Whitney U test. This is how you use it to calculate the level of significance for your data:

- Once you have entered each participant's score into a table (like the one above), you need to rank them. This means credit the smallest error as 1, the second smallest as 2, and so on until you reach the biggest error. If you have used 16 participants (8 in each group) you should have numbers between 1 and 16 next to each score.

- Add up all of the ranks for the participants who were shown the 45° fins (Ra) and all of the ranks for the participants who were shown the 60° fins (Rb). In the example given, $Ra = 75$ and $Rb = 61$.

- The number of participants you have used in group A is called Na; the number of participants in group B is called Nb.

- Put these four pieces of data into the following two formulae:

$$Ua = Na \times Nb + \frac{Na(Na + 1)}{2} - Ra \qquad Ub = Nb \times Na + \frac{Nb(Nb + 1)}{2} - Rb$$

Using the example data on page 12, the calculation for Ua would be:

$$Ua = 8 \times 8 + \frac{8(8 + 1)}{2} - 61$$

$$Ua = 64 + 36 - 61$$
$$Ua = 39$$

Hint

Before you insert your own figures, try working out the value of Ub from the example on page 12.

- Now use your own figures to work out the two values of Ua and Ub.

> *Using the smaller of the two values that you have calculated, you will compare this number with the table of critical values. We can refer to this number as* **U**. *Write the value of* **U** *that you have obtained here.*
>
> _____

Step 9 | *Interpret your results: is the result statistically significant?*

Assess whether the value of U that you have found is statistically significant or could have occurred by chance. Compare your observed value with the critical value taken from the table in the Appendix.

- Decide where to look in the table by finding N_1 and N_2. These refer to the number of participants looking at the 45° fins (N_1) and the number of participants looking at the 60° fins (N_2).

- The point in the table where these intersect is known as your critical value.

- Check whether you had a directional or non-directional hypothesis.

- If your result is equal to or less than the critical value, you can reject the null hypothesis and accept the alternative hypothesis. You have found a significant difference.

- If your result is larger than the critical value, you must retain the null hypothesis. Your data suggest there is no significant difference between the performance of the Müller-Lyer illusion when the fin angles are varied (45° or 60°).

- Complete the statistical conclusion below.

> *The observed value of* **U** = _____
>
> *This was* _____ *than the critical value of* _____
>
> *For* **N**$_1$ _____ *and* **N**$_2$ _____ *at a probability equal to 0.05.*
>
> *Therefore the null hypothesis was* _____

Critical discussion

Theory

- Did your findings support your hypothesis?
- If you retained the null hypothesis, can you think of reasons why this might be?
- Can you explain why the effect occurs more or less for a particular angle?

Methodology

- Did you have an appropriate number of participants?
- Was the illusion that you created clear enough?
- Were any of your participants familiar with the Müller-Lyer illusion already?
- Were your standardised instructions clear?

Ethics

- Did your study throw up any unseen ethical issues?
- How did your participants feel about taking part?
- What have you learned about research with people?

> **Thinking about validity**
>
> Could any participant variables have influenced the results (such as poor eyesight) or could any situational variables (such as low light levels) have made the illusion hard to see?

References

Dewar, R.E. (1967) Stimulus determinants of the magnitude of the Müller-Lyer illusion. *Perceptual and Motor Skills*, **24**, 708–10.

Howe, C.Q. and Purves, D. (2004) Size contrast and assimilation explained by the statistics of natural scene geometry. *Journal of Cognitive Neuroscience*, **16**, 90–102.

Restle, F. and Decker, J. (1977) Size of the Müller-Lyer illusion as a function of its dimensions: Theory and data. *Perception and Psychophysics*, **21**, 489–503.

Segall, M.H., Campbell, D.T. and Herskovits, M.J. (1963) Cultural differences in the perception of geometrical illusions. *Science*, **193**, 769–71.

Relationships

3 | The matching hypothesis

> **Learning outcomes for this practical**
> - A1, A2, A4, A5, B1, B3, B4, C1, C3, D2, E2, E5

Hint

Check these learning outcomes against the list on page iv.

Background

How important is physical attraction in relationships? Common sense suggests that physical appearance is an important factor in deciding who we choose as a partner. However, it also tells us that we cannot all end up with footballers or supermodels. In fact, most people happily settle for someone whose physical attractiveness is on a level similar to their own. This phenomenon was first noted by Murstein (1972) who put forward the idea of the matching hypothesis. Put simply, the matching hypothesis is the tendency to form a relationship with someone who has a similar level of attractiveness. This tendency to choose a similar partner is probably based on a fear of rejection. Although most of us would like a highly attractive partner, we tend to settle for someone fairly similar in order to avoid rejection. The following practical exercise involves testing Murstein's claim that couples have matching attractiveness.

Key study

Physical attractiveness and marital choice, Murstein (1972)

Murstein (1972) collected two sets of photographs of college students in order to test the claim that couples are matched in attractiveness. He used 99 photographs of people who were engaged to each other or in a serious long-term relationship. A further 98 photographs were of students who were not in a long-term or serious relationship.

Murstein then asked a sample of people or 'judges' to rate each photograph using a 5-point scale (with 0 being not attractive and 5 being very attractive) without knowing who was paired with who. He also asked the couples to rate their own and their partner's attractiveness.

Murstein compared the ratings given by the independent judges for the couples. He found that members of real couples received very similar ratings. In effect, people appeared to be paired up with someone who had a fairly similar level of attractiveness to themselves.

In the final part of the study, Murstein randomly paired up photographs of students and found – unsurprisingly – that there was little pattern in the attractiveness of the randomly paired couples.

> **Look it up ...**
>
> A variety of studies into the matching hypothesis have been carried out since Murstein put the theory forward. Familiarise yourself with some of these studies and refresh your memory about how the studies were carried out and what was found.

Method

Step 1 *Design your study: variables and hypotheses*

The first step of the research process is to identify a topic of interest and choose a suitable method to investigate it. Here, the topic of interest is the matching of couples on the basis of physical attractiveness, and you use a method that allows you to look for a correlation.

In a correlational study, the researcher does not manipulate an independent variable but measures two co-variables to establish whether there is a pattern or relationship between them. The two co-variables measured in this correlational study are:

- the attractiveness of the female member of a couple
- the attractiveness of her male partner.

You will need to measure between 10 and 20 couples to provide enough data to analyse. As you can see from the Key study box, Murstein asked a sample of independent judges to rate each photo using a 5-point scale. This kind of rating scale is called a Likert scale. In this exercise, you should use a 10-point scale to rate the photos.

Write the hypotheses for your study. The null hypothesis states that there will be no relationship between variable X and Y, whereas the experimental hypothesis predicts a relationship. You will need to decide whether your experimental hypothesis should be directional (use a one-tailed test) or non-directional (use a two-tailed test). Non-directional hypotheses are chosen when there is insufficient research to point to the outcome of the study or when previous research studies have produced conflicting results (that is, you do not know what the outcome will be).

> **Look it up ...**
>
> Refresh your memory about correlational studies and writing hypotheses by looking back at the research methods section in your A2 Student Book.

Write your hypotheses here.

- *Null hypothesis* _____

- *Alternative (experimental) hypothesis* _____

Justify your choice of a directional or non-directional hypothesis here:

I have chosen a _____ *hypothesis because* _____

_____

Step 2 *Sampling*

The photos

In this study you will have two samples. The first will be the people in the photographs who will be rated for attractiveness. The second sample group will be the judges who rate them. In order to generate sufficient data, use photographs of between 10 and 20 couples. Ensure that you use photos of couples who have been together for a reasonable period of time (around six months or more). There are a number of ways to obtain photos:

- Ask friends with a boyfriend/girlfriend if you can take photographs of them.
- Collect photographs from magazines or papers (e.g. wedding photos from the local paper).
- Collect photos of couples from the internet using websites or social networking sites.

Each of these methods poses its own set of ethical dilemmas. If photos are in a magazine or on a website, it will be impossible to ask for informed consent. However, when material is in the public arena (e.g. publicised wedding photos or magazine photos) you can assume that those involved have given their presumptive consent to be viewed, leaving you without that ethical dilemma.

If you decide to photograph people you know, you will need to ask for their consent. Before they agree to take part, you should give them as much information as possible about what will happen to the photos. Remember also that there may be further ethical problems when you ask other people to rate them – feelings can be easily hurt.

The judges

You will also have to choose a set of judges to rate the photos. Remember that judges *must* be over 16 and should – in theory – be a similar age to the people in the photographs. There are a few ways to choose the judges:

- a random sample
- an opportunity sample
- a self-selected (volunteer) sample.

You will also have to think about sample size. You will need to use between 10 and 20 judges to generate sufficient data. Aim for half male judges and half female judges in your sample. This mimics the actual population ratio of men and women and should balance out potential difficulties that heterosexual people might have with same-sex ratings of attractiveness.

> *Chosen sample method:*
>
> _____

Step 3 *Create stimulus materials, rating scales and data sheets*

Decide what kind of photos you intend to use. For the purposes of control, ensure that all of the photos are of a similar size and quality and they are either all in colour or all black and white. Standardise them in terms of face-only photos or full-body shots.

Think about how you present the photographs to your judges. Ensure that the males and females are separated so it is impossible to say who belongs with who. Three ways of doing this are shown in the table below. Think about the advantages and disadvantages of each of these procedures before making your decision.

Think about controls

If you decide to collect photos of couples from the internet using websites or social networking sites, how can you be sure that the couples have been together for six months or more?

Think about ethics

If you need to remind yourself about the importance of consent, look at the BPS ethical principles in the Appendix on page 91.

Look it up ...

Refresh your memory about the different methods of sampling by looking back at each of these in your A2 Student Book and thinking about the advantages and disadvantages of each.

Think about controls

Control is an important principle of research design. You need to ensure that stimulus materials and instructions are standardised as far as possible. How could different sizes/kinds of photos be important in this study?

Whichever procedure you decide on, each photo should be shown for the same length of time.

Method	Advantages	Problems
Present each photo on a separate sheet of A4 paper/card		
Put all of the female photographs together on A3 paper and all of the male photos together on another sheet of paper. Number each photo and ask your judges to rate each photo in turn		
If you have sourced photos on the internet, put them in a timed PowerPoint presentation		

Devise a set of standardised instructions for your judges that make it clear exactly what they need to do. Try to ensure that your instructions encourage your participants to use all of the numbers on the scale, not just the middle numbers.

Create a simple sheet to record your data on. This will contain lots of figures and will look quite complicated for a while, but there is no need to panic. The simplest way to do this is to take each photo and record all of the ratings given to it.

> **Hint**
>
> You may find that your instructions change after you have carried out your pilot study (Step 5). This is fine and it shows that your pilot has been useful.

Step 4 *Ethical issues*

Ethical issues guide practical choices and decisions at all stages of the research process. Think about the ethical issues involved in this piece of research.

- An important principle of research is to ensure that participants are able to give their fully informed consent to take part, knowing what they will be letting themselves in for. Tell potential participants what is involved in the study, what they will be asked to do and roughly how long it will take. Put this information on a consent form and ask the participants to sign it. You can view a sample consent form in the Appendix on page 92. The consent form should make it clear to your judges that they are free to withdraw at any time.

- Ensure that your research does not put your participants under stress or make them feel uncomfortable. You may find that some participants are reluctant to rate other people for physical attractiveness (especially those of the same sex). Some may feel uncomfortable doing this. Be sensitive to this when asking for consent and collecting your data.

■ Ensure participants are fully debriefed at the end of the study. Tell them what you expect to find and ask whether they have any questions. This is good ethical practice. Remember to thank every participant after they have taken part.

Step 5 *Pilot study*

A pilot study is the last stage of planning before real data are collected. It enables you to check that your materials, instructions and procedures work smoothly. Think about how and where you will collect your data. The environment you use should be kept the same for all of your participants (as far as is practically possible) so it can be ruled out as a variable. It should be relatively noise- and distraction-free. Make sure that you test people without others around to influence them. If you include photos of celebrities in your sample, ratings could be made on the basis of other attributes such as personality or whether the judge liked the character they played in their last film. Similarly, if you include photos of familiar people, for example from social networking sites, these could also be influenced by other factors than appearance. You need to control these extraneous variables or they could become confounding variables. Decide which photos (male or female) you will ask the judges to rate first. It is often a good idea to start with the photos of the opposite sex first (i.e. males rating females and vice versa) as many people feel more comfortable doing this. Then move on to same-sex ratings. Whatever you decide, you will need to be consistent in your approach.

Carry out a short pilot study testing three or four people to check that your materials and procedures work properly.

> **Think about controls**
>
> Aim to be consistent in respect of where, when and how your data are collected for the judges. Why do you think it is important to test people without their friends around?

Record any problems or changes needed to your procedure/instructions here.

_____

_____

Analysing your data

Step 6 *Organise and display your data*

You should have a completed data sheet with the scores given to each photo by all of your participants. Create a single score for each photograph. You can do this either by *totalling* the scores (which will give you relatively large numbers) or by calculating the *average score* given to each photo. Then you will need to 'reunite' the pictures of the couples so that you have the scores in pairs as shown in the table below. These will form the basis of your scattergram and your statistical analysis.

	Couple 1		Couple 2		Couple 3		Couple 4	
Sex	M	F	M	F	M	F	M	F
Average score	6.4	3.8	7.2	7.7	4.6	5.0	5.6	6.5

Plot these scores on a scattergram. Graphs provide an 'eyeball test' that shows at a glance the patterns or relationships in the data. In this case, your scattergram will help you to see whether there is a relationship between the scores given to the couples. Remember to give your graph a title and to label both axes appropriately. Your graph could be drawn on graph paper or presented using a computer program such as Word Excel. Look at your scattergram and compare it with the example below.

Scattergram

Attractiveness scores of males and females

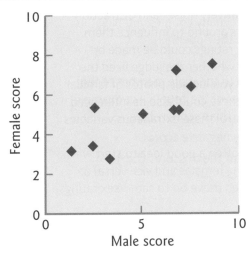

Describe the pattern shown by your data using the terms 'positive' or 'negative' correlation' and 'weak', 'moderate' or 'strong correlation' (or 'no correlation').

_____

Step 7 *Inferential statistics and testing for significance*

In order to test for significance, psychologists carry out statistical tests to show the likelihood that the relationship/difference obtained is real (significant) rather than occurring purely by chance. Choose your statistical test using a number of types of information, for example:

- What level of data was collected – nominal or ordinal?
- Did the research look for a difference between sets of data or a relationship between two variables?
- If an experiment has been carried out, what type of design was used?

> **Look it up …**
>
> You can refresh your memory about test choice using the flow chart in the Appendix.

Write down the statistical test you will use.

_____

Put your data into a table that looks like the table on page 22.

Couple	Male score	Rank	Female score	Rank	d	d^2
1	6.4	2	3.8	4	−2	4
2	7.2	1	7.7	1	0	0
3	4.6	4	5.0	3	1	1
4	5.6	3	6.5	2	1	1

- Rank the scores given to the male photos. Give the lowest score a rank of 1 and the highest a score a rank of 10 (or however many couples you have). If you have tied scores, give them a tied rank (see the Appendix).
- Repeat this process for the female scores.
- Find the difference (d) between the rank given to the male member of the couple and the rank given to the female member of the couple. For example, if the male is ranked 1 and the female is ranked 4, the d score will be −3.
- Square this difference, which will get rid of any negative scores.
- Add up the final column to calculate the total of the d^2 scores (Σd^2).

Put your data into the formula below:

$$r_s = 1 - \frac{6\Sigma d^2}{N(N^2 - 1)}$$

Work out the formula:

- Multiply (times) the total from the last column of your table (Σd^2) by 6.
- Take the number of couples in your sample (N) and multiply this by itself to find N^2. (If you had 10 couples $10 \times 10 = 100$)
- Multiply the number of couples in your sample by the squared value minus 1 (in the case of 10 couples, this would be 10×99) to find $N(N^2 - 1)$
- Take your answer for $6\Sigma d^2$ and divide this figure by $N(N^2 - 1)$
- Subtract the number in the previous step from 1.

You should now have a number between −1 and +1. A larger number (closer to +1 or −1) indicates a strong relationship, whereas a figure that is close to zero indicates a weak relationship.

- If the number is positive, this indicates a positive correlation.
- If the number is negative, this indicates a negative correlation.

This final number is your observed value of Spearman's rho. Write it here.

_____

Step 8 *Interpret your results. Is the result statistically significant?*

Assess whether the relationship you have found is statistically significant or could have occurred by chance. Compare your observed value with the critical value taken from the table in the Appendix.

- Decide where to look in the table by finding *N*. *N* refers to the number of couples used in your study.
- Check whether you had a directional or non-directional hypothesis (and so used a one- or a two-tailed test).
- Find the column for a probability level of 0.05.
- The point in the table where these intersect is known as your critical value.
- If your result is equal to or larger than the critical value, you can reject the null hypothesis and accept the alternative hypothesis. You have found a significant correlation.
- If your result is smaller than the critical value, you must retain the null hypothesis. Your data suggest there is no relationship between the attractiveness of the male and female members of your couples in this sample.
- Complete the statistical conclusion below.

The observed value of r_s = _____

This was _____ than the critical value of _____

for **N** = _____ probability equal to 0.05

Therefore the null hypothesis was _____

Critical discussion

Theory
- Did your findings support the matching hypothesis?
- If you retained the null hypothesis, can you think of reasons why this might be?
- Do you think that physical appearance plays less of a role in attraction than it did in 1972?

Methodology
- Did you have an appropriate number of photos and judges?
- Was the quality of the photos good enough? Were they presented for long enough?
- Was your rating scale a useful way of measuring attractiveness or could it have been improved?
- Were your standardised instructions clear?

Ethics
- Did your study produce any unseen ethical issues?
- How did your participants feel about taking part?
- What have you learned about research with people?

> **Think about validity**
>
> You could have carried out this study using pictures of celebrity couples. However, it would be very difficult to ensure that ratings of celebrities were made based only on appearance. Judges might rate them according to their personality or their last public appearance.

References

Murstein, B.I. (1972) Physical attractiveness and marital choice. *Journal of Personality and Social Psychology*, **22**(1), 8–12.

Aggression

4 Content analysis of children's television

Learning outcomes for this practical
- A1, A2, A5, B3, B4, C4, D1, D2

Hint

Check these learning outcomes against the list on page iv.

Background

Why do some people carry out aggressive behaviours that hurt others? There have been long debates about the causes of human aggression. Biological psychologists have argued that aggression is largely innate and have concentrated on searching for the biological underpinnings of aggressive behaviours. In contrast, behavioural psychologists have argued that experience and socialisation are important factors. It is likely that both of these things contribute to the development of aggression. While we may inherit the tendency to be more or less aggressive, upbringing and socialisation teaches us if or when the use of aggression is profitable or acceptable.

Bandura and colleagues carried out a series of studies of young children in the early 1960s. In the first of these, Bandura *et al.* (1963) demonstrated how 3- to 4-year-old children copied aggressive behaviours displayed by a role model towards an inflatable doll. In subsequent studies, Bandura found that children were more likely to imitate aggressive models who were rewarded in some way for their aggression. He also demonstrated that children would copy aggressive behaviour when it was directed at a real person – an adult dressed as a clown. From these studies, Bandura argued that children learn to behave aggressively through observation of role models: if aggressive behaviour is seen to bring rewards to a model, children are more likely to copy the behaviours they have seen (vicarious reinforcement). These simple ideas formed the basis of the social learning theory of aggression.

Bandura's studies implied that children will copy aggressive models seen in real life and on film, and his work led to an ongoing debate about possible effects of watching aggressive acts on television. Many TV programmes including news bulletins, reality shows, films and cartoons show a range of aggressive acts. Children are heavy consumers of television, watching an average of 2–3 hours a day. In one study of American television, Federman (1998) estimated that the average American child has seen around 200,000 violent acts and 16,000 murders on TV by the age of 18, with around two-thirds of all programming containing violence.

Content analyses of violence on TV

A number of studies have used content analysis to examine violence on television. In order to carry out such analyses, researchers have to think carefully how they intend to define and measure aggressive behaviour. For example, should physical force (e.g. pushing someone) or verbal violence (e.g. shouting or swearing) be included?

Hint

This exercise works best if you pair up with a partner so that you can collect more data and check that your coding system is reliable.

Ethical issues

Studies of human aggression involve considerable thought, skill and planning. They should be presented to ethics committees before researchers are permitted to carry them out. Studies of this nature are beyond the skills and expertise of A level psychologists. Remember that the prime ethical concern is to ensure that potential participants – and researchers – are protected from harm.

Wilson *et al.* (2002) examined the amount and types of violence shown in TV programmes that targeted American children under the age of 12. They defined violence as the intention to cause physical harm to an animate (living) being. Almost 3,000 television programmes targeted at children were recorded between October 1995 and June 1996 and the content was assessed for violence. These were compared with programmes targeted at adults.

Wilson *et al.* found that programmes targeted at children contained more violence than adult programmes: almost 70 per cent of children's shows contained some physical aggression, compared with around 60 per cent of non-children's shows. On average, one hour of children's programming contained 14 different violent incidents compared with around five incidents in non-children's programming. The violence itself was glamorised in both children's and adults' programmes, but violence was sanitised in children's TV.

Potter (1999) measured the amount of physical violence shown on prime-time TV and found that 60 per cent of programmes contained some violence. Potter also examined *how* violence was portrayed by looking at each act of violence and considering why it occurred, what kind of images were shown and the consequences that followed the violent act. Potter found that violence was used to achieve or gain something (such as power or property) in about 30 per cent of cases. In 58 per cent of the acts of violence shown, the victim was not shown suffering any harm and 37 per cent of the violent acts showed no punishment for the perpetrator by the end of the programme. Almost 40 per cent of the acts of violence were shown in a humorous way. Like Wilson *et al.*, Potter also found minimal coverage of the 'blood and guts' in the physical violence.

These studies suggest that acts of physical aggression and violence are commonplace in children's television programmes. Your task is to use the method of content analysis to examine the amount of violence depicted in children's television and the ways in which violence is portrayed. For the purpose of this exercise, you should focus on programmes aimed at older children (called 'tweenies') aged between about 9 and 13.

Method

Step 1 *Research questions*

Content analysis is a method designed to examine materials such as books, TV programmes and newspapers. It is often used in media studies to investigate how topics are portrayed and represented. The aim of this piece of practical work is to collect descriptive data that show how violence is depicted in television programmes aimed at children. The data collected will not be suited to statistical testing, but it can be displayed in the form of percentages.

In this study, there is no attempt to control variables or to look for differences or correlations. It is inappropriate to include a hypothesis for two reasons:

- A hypothesis refers to the effects of an independent variable on a dependent variable.
- A hypothesis makes a prediction regarding a difference or association.

> **Look it up …**
>
> You may want to remind yourself about the differences between a hypothesis and a research question by looking back at your A2 Student Book.

In work of this nature, a more open research question can be used to guide the analysis. Here, we would like you to address two research questions:

■ How much violence is there in children's TV programmes?

■ How is violence portrayed in children's TV programmes?

Step 2 *Operational definitions*

In order to measure anything, we must first decide how we intend to define or operationalise it. You will notice that most of the studies covered above measured violence rather than aggressive behaviour. One reason for this is that aggression is a more subjective term that is open to interpretation. Behaviours such as spreading rumours, teasing or posting unflattering photos on the internet could all be classed as aggressive as they intend to hurt someone. However, violence relates to a clear physical act aimed at causing physical rather than emotional harm. **Think about the different kinds of behaviour that might be classed as violence. Write your initial thoughts down here.**

> **Look it up …**
>
> Refresh your memory about the importance of operational definitions by looking back at the methods section in your A2 Student Book.

Examples of violent behaviour:

_____

_____

_____

Compare your thoughts with your working partner's definition. Which elements seem to be common?

_____

_____

_____

Violence could include many different kinds of behaviour such as physical force (e.g. pushing) verbal violence (e.g. shouting or swearing) as well as more obvious behaviour such as hitting, kicking, and so on. As we noted above, Wilson *et al.* defined violence as the intention to cause physical harm to an animate (living) being. In their study an act was classed as violent if it:

■ was deliberate not accidental

■ caused physical damage to the victim

■ was directed at a human or animal that could feel pain.

Write down your own operational definition of violence here.

_____

_____

_____

_____

Step 3 Select a representative sample of TV programmes

There are a large number of TV channels showing lots of programmes. You will need to choose a sample of programmes that are aimed at 9- to 13-year-old children. Your sample should be selected in an unbiased way and be representative of the different kinds of programmes aimed at children. Select your sample using the following steps:

- Decide on the number of different channels you will include. You could focus on terrestrial channels (BBC 1 and BBC 2, ITV, Channels 4 and 5), cable and satellite channels or a mixture of both. Whichever you decide, you should ensure that you have programmes from four channels to analyse.

- Make a list of all the programmes on your chosen channels that are shown between 4.30pm and 7.30pm Monday to Friday. Children return home from school at this time, so many of the programmes in this slot are aimed at them. This should give you 15 hours of television per channel. Multiplied by four channels, this is 60 hours of TV programmes in total. It is not feasible in the course of this research to watch and code a whole 60 hours' worth of programmes. We need to find a way of watching a representative sample of what will be shown. If a particular programme is on every day and another is on only once a week, we should watch and code five times more of the daily programme than the weekly programme.

- Look at the programmes on your list and categorise them into types (or 'genres'). Common genres include news programmes, cartoons, films, soap operas, quiz shows, programmes about animals, and drama. You may find additional categories to these along with some programmes that do not seem to fit in any category and which should be classed as 'other'. Give each programme a code to indicate which genre it belongs to.

- Calculate the amount of time each programme is on TV over the five-day period and put this into a table similar to the one below.

Name of programme	Genre	Total time over week
The Simpsons	Cartoon	150 mins
Newsround	News	75 mins
Hollyoaks	Drama	150 mins
Neighbours	Soap	150 mins

- Now, calculate the total amount of time for each genre across the whole week using all channels. Put these totals into a summary table similar to the one below. You will watch and code 10 per cent of each genre of programmes. Divide the total time for each genre by 10 to work out what is 10 per cent of the total time. These will be selected so that your sample resembles the proportions of programmes in the overall output. This is a form of sampling known as stratified sampling.

Genre	Total time over the week	10% of the actual time
Cartoon	650 mins	65 mins
News	300 mins	30 mins
Drama	300 mins	30 mins
Soap	450 mins	45 mins

Step 4 *Devise a coding system and carry out a pilot study*

Next you need to decide how you will code the data. Carry out some pilot work with your partner. Select a couple of children's programmes that will not be in your final sample. Watch the first one together and discuss each violent act as it happens. Remember to refer back to your definition of violence and ensure that each act fits your criteria. You may decide that some acts are better categorised as violent episodes (e.g. a fight scene that cannot be split up into separate acts).

Now discuss how each act of violence is portrayed. Each act is likely to involve three elements: a perpetrator (someone who acted out the violent behaviour), a target (a person who was the victim) and the actual act of violence itself. For each act, you could discuss and record the following kinds of information (these were used in the studies by Potter and Wilson *et al.*):

- who carried out the violence (age/sex)
- who was the victim (age/sex)
- whether the violence was punished in any way
- whether the punishment was immediate or occurred later
- whether the scene showed any negative consequences for the victim (blood, pain)
- what led to or provoked the violence
- whether the violence was shown humorously.

When you have worked your way through the first programme, you and your partner should code the second programme separately from each other with no discussion. After you have done this, get back together and compare your answers. If you are in close agreement, you can continue with your main data collection. If there are serious disagreements, you will need to replay the programme and discuss the incidents that have led to disagreement and decide how they will be categorised.

Step 5 *Data collection*

Now you can watch and code the remaining set of programmes in your sample. You may find it easiest to divide them between yourself and your working partner so you both watch about three hours of TV. You might need to watch programmes several times. You can use an internet site such as iPlayer or another channel's dedicated website to view programmes, where you can pause the broadcast in order to re-watch and record your findings. You may be able to use other devices to record the programmes, and these will give you the ability to time, pause and rewind the programmes to allow you to code them effectively. Record your data for each programme using a data sheet similar to the example below.

Name of programme _____

Date broadcast _____

Genre _____

Incident number	1	2	3	4	5
Who carried out the violence (age/sex)	Male aged 15	Female aged 16			
Who was the victim (age/sex)	Male 13	Male 16			
Was the violence punished in any way?	Yes	No			
Was punishment immediate or later?	Later				
Did the scene show any negative consequences for the victim (e.g. blood, pain)?	No	Blood on face			
What provoked the violence?	Getting own back	Jealousy			
Was the violence shown humorously?	No	No			

Step 6 *Summarise and display your data*

Research question 1: How much violence is there in children's TV programmes?

You should have a completed data sheet for each programme that you watched. Summarise the main findings of your study using descriptive statistics. For the first research question (How much violence is on TV?), you should calculate the total number of violent acts for each genre and the average number of violent acts per hour. Put these into a table like the one on page 30. You can also display these findings using a bar chart.

Type of programme	Total number of violent acts	Rate of violent acts per hour
Drama	3	6
Cartoon	13	12

Bar chart
Rate of violent acts per hour

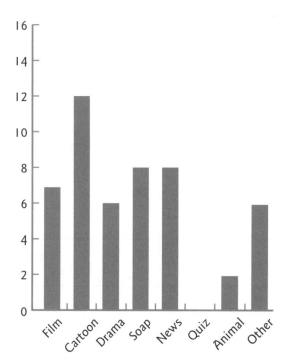

Comment on your findings for research question 1.

> *Which types of programme included the highest and the lowest number of violent incidents?*
>
> _____
>
> _____

Research question 2: How is violence portrayed in children's TV programmes?

Now look at the data you have collected on the context surrounding violence.
Summarise the key findings of your data. Put your answer in a table like the one below.

Findings	
Perpetrators of violence	*68% male and 32% female. Mainly young (under 20)*
Victims of violence	*46% male and 54% female*
Percentage of violent acts that were punished	*30% were punished*

Critical discussion

Theory and research

- How do these findings compare with Wilson's claim that 70 per cent of children's shows contain violence?
- Heymann found that cartoons were particularly violent. Did your content analysis support this claim?
- Potter found that victims were not depicted suffering harm in about 60 per cent of cases. How did your findings compare?
- Do you agree with Wilson's claim that there is minimal coverage of the blood and guts involved in physical violence and that violence is sanitised?
- How is violence portrayed in news programmes?

Methodology

- How well did your sampling system work?
- Were there programmes that were difficult to classify in terms of genre?
- Do you think there may be differences in content between American and British programmes? How could you test this?
- How reliable was your system of coding violent acts? How could you have made this more reliable?

Ethics

- Did this study produce any unforeseen effects on you?
- What do you think are the main ethical issues in content analyses of this nature?

References

Bandura, A. Ross, D. and Ross, S.A (1963) Imitation of film mediated aggressive models. *Journal of Abnormal and Social Psychology*, **66**, 3–11.

Federman, J. (1998) *National Television Violence Study, Vol. 3*. Thousand Oaks, CA: Sage.

Potter, W.J. (1999) On media violence. In D. Giles (2003) *Media Psychology*. New Jersey: Lawrence Erlbaum.

Wilson, B.J., Smith, S.L., Potter, W.J., Kunkel, D., Linz, D.U., Colvin, C.M. and Donnerstein, E. (2002) Violence in children's television programming: Assessing the risks. *Journal of Communication*, **52**(1), 5–35.

Eating behaviour

5 Sex differences and body image

Learning outcomes for this practical

- A1, A2, A4, A5, B1, B3, B4, C1, C2, C3, C5, D2, E3, E5

Hint

Check these learning outcomes against the list on page iv.

Background

The eating disorders anorexia and bulimia nervosa are far more prevalent in women than men. It has been suggested that one reason for this might be the sheer volume of idealised figures displayed in magazines and on television or in films – beautiful women are portrayed as slim. The idealised male figure is not similarly portrayed. If anything, an attractive man is more likely to be depicted as muscular.

Fallon and Rozin (1985) used silhouettes of male and female shapes to investigate sex differences relating to body image, and found that women were a lot more unhappy with their body shape than men. It has also been noted that this dissatisfaction is a relatively recent phenomenon. In the 1940s it was found that thin people were associated with negative personality traits, whereas by the 1980s thin people were considered the most desirable (Turner *et al.*, 1997). Garner *et al.* (1980) found that the winners of Miss America and the models in *Playboy* have become increasingly smaller (judged by bust and hip sizes) since 1959. On the other hand, the shape of male icons has not changed at all.

This may be what has led to the discrepancy between the number of male and female sufferers of anorexia and bulimia. As slim women are thought to be more attractive, an increasing number of women want to be slim and this has led to increasing body dissatisfaction among women.

Key study

Differences in body image between men and women, Prevos (2005)

Previous research had conflicting results, and society's views of beauty had changed over time, so in 2005 Prevos conducted an up-to-date study to investigate what men and women thought about their bodies. Using 59 male and 107 female participants, he showed a series of body shapes to each person and asked them to identify first their current shape and then their ideal shape. The difference between these two shapes constituted 'body dissatisfaction'.

It was found that women's ideal shape was usually thinner than their actual shape, and consequently they felt a certain amount of body dissatisfaction. The men's ideal shape was much closer to their actual shape. (This was similar to the results of Fallon and Rozin in 1985.) Some 66 per cent of women wanted to be thinner than they were, and 38 per cent of men wanted to be thinner than they were.

There were two other interesting findings:

- the female body shape that men find most attractive is larger than women's own ideal
- as age increases, so too does the size of ideal body shape for both men and women.

Although the participants in this research were students, it must be remembered that half of them were over 30, which is why Prevos was able to draw conclusions about age differences as well as sex differences.

Method

Step 1 *Design your study: variables and hypotheses*

The point of this study is to investigate whether sex has an impact on how we perceive our actual body shape and our ideal body shape. You will try to obtain the answers to these two questions from your participants. The discrepancy between the two answers will constitute each participant's body dissatisfaction.

Strictly speaking, this is known as a quasi experiment because it is impossible for the experimenter to manipulate the independent variable. In this study, a participant is either male or female, and it would not be possible for the researcher to randomly allocate participants to either condition. However, in all other respects this study follows the conventions of normal experiments.

You will need to identify an independent variable and a dependent variable:

- The independent variable is sex.
- The dependent variable is the difference between participants' actual body shape and their ideal body shape, measured by a numerical score.

Many people use the terms 'sex' and 'gender' interchangeably, but the two words mean different things. Our participants have been divided into groups of males and females. This is a biological difference, and so the independent variable has to be sex. If we find a significant difference between the males and females in terms of their views about their bodies, we might conclude that this is a behavioural difference, and therefore a difference of gender.

Write the hypotheses for your study. The null hypothesis states that the independent variable will have no effect on the dependent variable, whereas the experimental hypothesis predicts there will be an effect. You will need to decide whether your experimental hypothesis should be directional (use a one-tailed test) or non-directional (use a two-tailed test). Non-directional hypotheses are chosen when there is insufficient research to point to the outcome of the study or when previous research studies have produced conflicting results (i.e. you do not know what the outcome will be).

Write your hypotheses here:

- *Null hypothesis* _____

- *Alternative (experimental) hypothesis* _____

Justify your choice of a directional or non-directional hypothesis here:

I have chosen a _____ *hypothesis because* _____

_____

Step 2 *Create your apparatus*

Photocopy and print out the picture of the different body outlines on page 98 in the Appendix. It might be an idea to separate the pictures of men from the pictures of women, and show each participant only the one set of images that relates to him or her. The figures need to be big enough to be clearly distinguishable. As you will be handing this out to lots of people, you might want to ask if it can be laminated.

Step 3 *The procedure*

Once you have made your apparatus, you need to follow this procedure:

- Devise a set of standardised instructions to read to each participant.
- Ask each participant to look at the set of figure outlines and to identify which number figure is the closest to how they think of their own body shape.
- When they have done this, ask them to identify which figure represents their ideal shape (what they would like to look like).
- Subtract the first number (actual shape) from the second number (ideal shape) and you will find the participant's body dissatisfaction.
- If the participant would like to be thinner than they are, the number will be negative. If they want to be larger, the number will be positive. If the participant is happy with their body size, the two figures will match and the calculation will produce a zero.

Write this figure in a table, ready to perform your statistical analysis.

Step 4 *Sampling*

In this study, you will need approximately the same number of male and female participants. Although it does not have to be exactly the same number in each group, having a similar number will improve the validity of your study. There are a few different ways that you might obtain your participants:

- random sampling
- opportunity sampling
- self-selecting (volunteer) sampling.

Ethical issues

Remember that your participants *must* be at least 16 years old. So if you decide to use your school friends, do not use children from classes below your own.

Decide whether to use a very simple method of obtaining participants or, if you think participant variables might be an issue, whether to ensure the sample is representative by using a more complicated method. Also, you should decide how many people are required. You need enough to increase the chances of your results being statistically significant, but not so many that your calculations are difficult.

Look it up ...

Refresh your memory about the different methods of sampling by looking back at each method in your A2 Student Book and thinking about the advantages and disadvantages of each.

Step 5 *Ethical issues*

Ethical issues guide practical choices and decisions at all stages of the research process.

- An important principle of research is to ensure that participants are able to give their fully informed consent to take part, knowing what they will be letting themselves in for. Tell potential participants what is involved in the study, what they will be asked to do and roughly how long it will take. Put this information on a consent form and ask the participants to sign it. You can view a sample consent form in the Appendix on page 92. The consent form should make it clear that the participants are free to withdraw at any time.

- Ensure that your research does not put your participants under stress or make them feel uncomfortable. If people feel embarrassed about the shape of their own bodies, they might be reluctant to answer the type of questions you will be asking. People may be sensitive about body shape. Be aware of this, and conduct your study carefully.

- Maintain confidentiality. The participants must not be identifiable. A good way to deal with this is to give each participant a number or code, e.g. P1, P2, P3 and so on. Initials or names should be avoided.

- Ensure participants are fully debriefed at the end of the study. Tell them what you expect to find and ask whether they have any questions. This is good ethical practice. Remember to thank all of the participants after they have taken part.

Step 6 *Piloting*

A pilot study is the last stage of planning, before real data are collected. It enables you to check that your materials, instructions and procedures work smoothly. Think about how and where you will collect your data. The environment you use should be kept the same (as far as is practically possible) for all of the participants, so it can be ruled out as a variable. This should be relatively noise- and distraction-free (e.g. no mobile phones interrupting the procedure). Other variables that you need to consider are demand characteristics. It is important that your participants do not try to alter their answers to provide the results they think you are looking for. For this reason, you should not provide them with your hypothesis in advance. Make sure that you test people without others around to influence them or see their responses. Make sure the participants understand what they are supposed to do, and can see the outline figures clearly.

Carry out a short pilot study testing three or four people to check that your materials and procedures work smoothly.

Think about controls

Are there any extraneous variables you should control or randomise so they do not systematically affect the responses of males or females? Might the sex of the investigator affect participant responses?

Think about controls

Aim to be consistent in relation to where, when and how your data are collected. Why do you think it is important to test people without their friends around?

Analysing your data

Step 7 *Organise and display your data*

You should have a completed data sheet with the difference between each participant's actual body shape and his or her ideal body shape. This difference (if any) is referred to as the discrepancy. The table should also include the ranks of each score, which are explained in step 8 below.

Put your data into a table like the one below.

Male participants (Group A)	Discrepancy	Rank	Female participants (Group B)	Discrepancy	Rank
A1	−1	6.5	B1	−2	3.0
A2	0	10.5	B2	0	10.5
A3	0	10.5	B3	−1	6.5
A4	−2	3.0	B4	−3	1.0
A5	1	13.5	B5	−2	3.0
A6	2	15.0	B6	0	10.5
A7	−1	6.5	B7	−1	6.5
A8	3	16.0	B8	1	13.5
	Mean = +0.25	81.5		**Mean = −1**	54.5

The mean figures should be taken as an indication of the general tendencies. This is done by adding up the numbers and dividing by the total in the group. You can plot a bar graph to show the means of the two groups.

Step 8 *Inferential statistics and testing for significance*

In order to test for significance, psychologists carry out statistical tests to show the likelihood that the relationship/difference obtained is real (significant) rather than occurring purely by chance. Choose your statistical test using a number of types of information:

- What level of data was collected – nominal or ordinal?
- Did the research look for a difference between sets of data or a relationship between two variables?
- If an experiment has been carried out, what type of design was used?

Write down the statistical test you will use.

_____

If you have answered the three questions above correctly, you will have arrived at the Mann-Whitney U test. This is how you use it to calculate the level of significance for your data:

- Once you have entered each participant's score in a table (such as the one above), you need to rank them. This means that you credit the lowest figure as 1, the second lowest as 2, and so on until you reach the highest figure. You need to rank all the scores as if all the participants were one group, so if you have used 16 participants (8 in each group), you should have numbers between 1 and 16 next to each score.

- Add up all of the ranks for the male participants (Ra) and all of the ranks for the female participants (Rb). In the table on page 36, $Ra = 81.5$ and $Rb = 54.5$.

- The number of participants you have used in group A is called Na. The number of participants in group B is called Nb.

- Put these four pieces of data into the following two formulae:

$$Ua = Na \times Nb + \frac{Na(Na + 1)}{2} - Ra$$

$$Ub = Nb \times Na + \frac{Nb(Nb + 1)}{2} - Rb$$

In the example on page 36:

$$Ua = 8 \times 8 + \frac{8(8 + 1)}{2} - 81.5$$

$$Ua = 64 + 36 - 81.5$$
$$Ua = 18.5$$

> **Hint**
>
> Before you insert your own figures, try working out the value of Ub from the example on page 36.

- Now use your own figures to work out the two values of Ua and Ub.

*Using the smaller of the two values that you have calculated, you will compare this number with the table of critical values. We can refer to this number as **U**. Write the value of **U** that you have obtained here.*

_____

Step 9 *Interpret your results: is the result statistically significant?*

Assess whether the value of U that you have found is statistically significant or could have occurred by chance. Compare your observed value with the critical value taken from the table in the Appendix.

- Decide where to look in the table by finding N_1 and N_2. These refer to the number of male participants (N_1) and the number of female participants (N_2).
- The point in the table where these intersect is known as your critical value.
- Check whether you had a directional or a non-directional hypothesis.
- If your result is equal to or less than the critical value, you can reject the null hypothesis and accept the alternative hypothesis. You have found a significant difference.
- If your result is larger than the critical value, you must retain the null hypothesis. Your data suggest there is no significant difference between the body dissatisfaction of males and females.
- Complete the statistical conclusion below.

> *The observed value of **U** = _____*
>
> *This was _____ than the critical value of _____*
>
> *showing a probability of _____ equal to 0.05*
>
> *Therefore the null hypothesis was _____*

Think about validity

Could any participant variables have influenced the results, such as low self-esteem or distorted body image (a characteristic of anorexia)? Or could demand characteristics have influenced your participants' answers? Either of these factors could affect the validity of your findings.

Critical discussion

Theory

- Did your findings support your hypothesis?
- Did the findings support previous research?
- If you retained the null hypothesis, can you think of reasons why this might be?
- Do you think this shows there are sex differences in body dissatisfaction?

Methodology

- Did you have an appropriate number of participants?
- Were any of them too embarrassed to give honest answers?
- Were your standardised instructions clear?

Ethics

- Did your study throw up any unseen ethical issues?
- How did your participants feel about taking part?
- What have you learned about research with people?

References

Fallon, A.E. and Rozin, P. (1985) Sex differences in perceptions of desirable body shape. *Journal of Abnormal Psychology*, **94**, 102–5.

Garner, D.M., Garfinkel, P.E., Schwarz, D. and Thompson, M. (1980) Cultural expectations of thinness in women. *Psychological Reports*, **47**, 483–91.

Prevos, P. (2005) Differences in body image between men and women. http://prevos.net/ola/body_image.pdf.

Turner, S., Hamilton, H., Jacobs, M., Angood, L.M. and Dwyer, D.H. (1997) The influence of fashion magazines on the body image satisfaction of college women: an exploratory analysis. *Adolescence*, **32**(127), 603–14.

Gender

6 Investigating the link between handwriting and 2D:4DR

Learning outcomes for this practical

- A1, A2, A4, A5, B1, B2, B3, B4, C1, C3, D2, E2

Hint

Check these learning outcomes against the list on page iv.

Background

There is an ongoing debate about how people develop gender role behaviours. Biological psychologists take the view that gender role behaviours result from a person's physical sex. According to this approach, men act in a masculine way because of the action of male hormones on the brain and the body; women act in a feminine way because they lack male hormones. This position is hotly disputed by psychologists on the nurture side of the debate who argue that gender roles are learned through socialisation. Girls become feminine and boys become masculine because they are given rewards for gender-appropriate behaviour and they are punished for gender-inappropriate behaviour. They are also brought up in a media-saturated world filled with role models on TV and in magazines showing different images of masculinity and femininity.

How can we examine the importance of hormones in the acquisition of gender role behaviours? Psychologists have used a variety of sources of evidence to do this. Animal experiments have been carried out in which female rats have been exposed to exceptionally high levels of male hormones and have developed masculine behaviours (Young, 1964) Case studies of girls exposed prenatally to high levels of male hormones have shown some differences in behaviour, with girls preferring more boyish games. These studies have serious ethical considerations and are carried out only by experienced researchers.

Other researchers have used physiological markers, that is, bodily features, which are associated with hormone exposure. One of the most widely used of these is 2D:4DR. This stands for second to fourth digit ratio and relates to the relative sizes of the second (index) and fourth (ring) fingers. It is calculated by measuring the second (index) finger and dividing this by the length of the fourth (ring) finger. Men generally have a longer ring finger than index finger, giving them 2D:4DR score of less than 1. Women typically have a longer index finger than ring finger, giving them a score of more than 1.

Finger length is related to exposure to testosterone in the womb. Boys are generally exposed to greater amounts of testosterone and have longer ring fingers than index fingers. Girls are generally exposed to less testosterone and have longer index fingers than ring fingers.

2D:4DR research studies

A variety of studies have been carried out into 2D:4DR and these have produced rather contradictory results. Rammsayer and Troche (2007) carried out a study using a sample of 423 male and 312 female university students. Each student was asked to complete Bem's SRI, a questionnaire that measures masculinity and femininity. The scores from the SRI put each student into one of four categories: masculine, feminine, androgynous (scoring highly on both masculine and feminine scales) or undifferentiated (not scoring highly on either scale).

2D:4DR

Next, each participant had their hands measured to calculate their 2D:4DR. Rammsayer and Troche correlated the scores for masculinity with the finger measurement, then repeated the correlation exercise for femininity. They found that men who had higher scores on the femininity scale had a 2D:4DR pattern that was characteristic of women, with a longer index finger than ring finger. This implied that more feminine men may have experienced lower exposure to male hormones in the womb. This study is ethically sensitive. Gender role behaviours may be linked to sexuality; both gender and sexuality are personal and private topics.

In order to investigate the link between hormone exposure and gender in a less ethically sensitive way, Beech and Mackintosh (2005) decided to use a different measurement of gender. Boys and girls often have different writing styles. Instead of measuring masculinity and femininity using a scale, Beech and Mackintosh chose to measure handwriting. The researchers selected a sample of 120 male and female students and asked them to provide a sample of their usual handwriting under controlled conditions. They were supplied with lined paper and identical black handwriting pens and asked to write the same sentence, which contained all the letters of the alphabet. The handwriting samples were then put to a panel of 20 judges (other students) who were asked to give each writing sample a score, from 1 to 5. A score of 1 was awarded to handwriting that was judged to be 'definitely male' and 5 was awarded to a writer who was 'definitely female'. The judges correctly identified the gender of two-thirds of the writers.

Following this, Beech and Mackintosh measured the 2D:4DR of each participant. They then correlated the scores from the handwriting sample with the 2D:4DR score. They found a significant positive correlation between the variables. Those with more female fingers had more feminine handwriting.

> **Look it up …**
>
> A variety of studies have been carried out into the relationships between gender role behaviour and 2D:4DR. Familiarise yourself with some of these studies using your A2 Student Book. Refresh your memory about how the study was carried out and what was found. You can find out about more of these studies using internet sources.

Method

Step 1 *Designing your study: Variables and hypotheses*

The first step of the research process is to identify a topic of interest and to choose a suitable method to investigate it. Here, the topic of interest is the possible relationship between biological markers of hormone exposure, specifically 2D:4DR, and a very specific aspect of gender role behaviour – handwriting. We are going to use correlational analysis, the method used by Beech and Mackintosh (2005).

In a correlational study, the researcher does not manipulate an independent variable but measures co-variables to establish whether there is a pattern or relationship between them. In this correlational study, we are going to use the two co-variables used by Beech and Mackintosh. These are:

- the 2D:4DR of a set of participants
- the handwriting of these participants.

> **Look it up …**
>
> Refresh your memory about correlational studies by looking back at the relevant section in your A2 Student Book.

Different ways of measuring the length of fingers include using a ruler, lined graph paper or callipers (you may be able to borrow these from a biology department). Think about the advantages and disadvantages of each of these methods. Try out some of these methods (and any more you can think of) and choose the method that produces the clearest and most accurate and consistent measurement of fingers.

You need to measure the handwriting of your participants. Two possible methods include asking for a sample of their writing (e.g. from a set of A level notes) or asking them to write something specific for your study in controlled conditions. Beech and Mackintosh used the second of these methods. Try to identify why they chose that method by thinking about the advantages and disadvantages of each. Fill in the table.

> **Think about controls**
>
> Consider whether using existing handwriting or handwriting under controlled conditions might give rise to extraneous variables.

	Existing sample	Writing under controlled conditions
Advantages		
Disadvantages		

You will need to rate the handwriting samples for femininity/masculinity. Use the same 5-point scale as Beech and Mackintosh with a score of 1 meaning definitely male and 5 meaning definitely female.

Write the hypotheses for your study. The null hypothesis states that there will be no relationship between the co-variables and the experimental hypothesis predicts a relationship. Decide whether your experimental hypothesis should be directional (one-tailed) or non-directional (two-tailed). Non-directional hypotheses are chosen when there is insufficient research to point to the outcome of the study or when previous research is contradictory. Remember that for this kind of study, a directional hypothesis would use the terms 'positive correlation' or 'negative correlation'.

Write your hypotheses here.

■ *Null hypothesis* _____

■ *Alternative (experimental) hypothesis* _____

Justify your choice of a directional or non-directional hypothesis here:

I have chosen a _____ *hypothesis because* _____

_____

Step 2 *Sampling*

The study will have two groups of participants. The first group will supply both sets of data (the handwriting sample and the 2D:4DR score). In order to generate sufficient data to analyse, you should use a sample of between 15 and 20 adults. It is also important that you have equal numbers of male and female participants in your sample. Remember that participants *must* be adults aged over 16. In this study, it is also important that they are able and willing to write. You can select them using a variety of sampling methods:

- a random sample
- an opportunity sample
- a self-selected (volunteer) sample.

Chosen sample method:

_____

You will also need a set of people to rate the handwriting. Beech and Mackintosh used a panel of 20 judges, but you may decide to use fewer than this. Five would be sufficient, but you can choose more if they are available. You should use the same judges for all of the handwriting samples. The judges should not see the measuring and handwriting task nor should they know the sex of the participants' handwriting before they rate it.

Step 3 *Ethical issues*

Think about the ethical issues involved in your research. This is a sensitive area and you should be aware that participants may feel they are being judged based on the quality of their writing.

- Ask for consent from your participants. This should be done by drafting a consent form, which you present to all of the participants to sign. This should make it clear that their handwriting will be rated by other people, but it will be anonymous so they will not know whose writing it is. Reassure the participants that this is not a test of their intelligence and that you are looking for patterns, not judging individuals. You can view a sample consent form in the Appendix on page 92. The consent form should make it clear to the participants that they are free to withdraw from the study at any time.

- Ask for consent from your group of judges. Again, you should give them clear information about what they will be asked to do and how long this will take.

- Ensure that you keep all of the information about the identity of your participants confidential. The handwriting samples should be labelled with numbers or initials that make it impossible for the judges to identify who produced them.

Look it up ...

If you need to refresh your memory about the BPS ethical principles, you can look at these in the Appendix.

Ethical issues

We often assume that everyone can read and write easily – but 5 million adults in the UK struggle with literacy. Do not put people under pressure to take part and do not ask for a reason if they refuse.

- Ensure participants are fully debriefed. Tell them what you expect to find and ask whether they have any questions. Make sure this explains that their data will be anonymous, that people will be judging whether they think the handwriting is from a male or female participant, and that some researchers think that finger length is related to handwriting. Answer any of their questions. This is good ethical practice. Thank all of the participants after they have taken part.

Step 4 *Design stimulus materials, rating scales and data sheets*

Think about how you will collect your data. Decide which of the two tasks – writing or finger measuring – will be carried out first. The order should be kept the same for all of your participants.

Decide what you want your participants to write. You could choose a single sentence or a short passage taken from a book. Previous researchers have chosen sentences that use every letter of the alphabet such as: 'The quick brown fox jumped over the lazy dog'. Have a look at some samples of these on the internet and choose a sentence that should not pose too many spelling challenges for your participants. Present your chosen sentence or passage to your participants in word-processed format. Make sure that you choose a font that is easily readable in a suitable size.

> **Think about validity**
>
> Why might the following sentence be unsuitable?
> Ebenezer unexpectedly bagged two tranquil aardvarks with his jiffy vacuum cleaner.

Look back at the description of Beech and Mackintosh's study and list the controls they used to collect the writing sample and why they used those controls. Use the same controls in your own study, together with any others you see as important.

Controls used:

_____

_____

_____

Design a set of standardised instructions for your participants. This should tell them clearly what you want them to do.

Create a data sheet similar to the one below on which to record your data. This will need to include the measurements of both fingers and the scores given by your judges for each handwriting sample. Make a note against the participant number to show whether they are male or female.

Participant	2nd finger	4th finger	Handwriting ratings				
1 F	63 mm	67mm	5	3	4	5	2
2M	72mm	68mm	4	2	1	2	2

Step 5 *Piloting*

Your pilot study is the last stage of planning before data are collected. Carry out a short pilot study testing three or four people on the handwriting and measuring tasks to check that your materials, instructions and procedures work smoothly. Think about the environment you use. This should be relatively noise- and distraction-free. Make sure that you test people without others around to influence them. The type of pen or paper used and the sentence that you ask your participants to write needs to be kept consistent. If these factors are not kept consistent, they may become confounding variables.

Pilot your rating scale. You may find it easiest to gather two or three judges together and pass each sample around identified only by a number or code. (Do *not* imply the participants' sex on the code!). Check whether the instructions and the rating scale are clear. These precautions may allow you to use this piloting data as part of the final data sample if your method is successful and does not need to be adjusted as a result of the pilot.

Analysing your data

Step 6 *Organise and display your data*

After you have collected all your data, you should have a completed data sheet. This will contain the finger measurements and the ratings given to each sample of handwriting. This raw data will need to be converted into two scores representing each of your variables.

- Create a single score for each handwriting sample. Do this by totalling the scores, then calculating the average rating given to each sample by dividing this by the number of judges.
- Calculate the 2D:4DR score using the following formula:

    2D:4DR = length of 2nd finger divided by length of 4th finger

For example:

Participant 1 had an index finger that was 70 mm long and ring finger that was 72 mm long.

$$70 \div 72 = 0.972$$

The second data sheet should have both scores (the actual ratios and the average handwriting scores) in pairs, as shown below. These will form the basis of your scattergram and your statistical analysis.

Participant	Sex	2D:4DR score	Handwriting score
I	F	0.940	4.0
2	M	I.059	2.2

The first stage of analysis is to plot these scores on a scattergram. This will help you to see whether there is a relationship between the 2D:4DR score and the ratings given to the handwriting sample. It will also provide an 'eyeball test' that will show you at a glance any patterns within the data. Remember to give your graph a title and to label both axes appropriately. Your graph could be drawn on graph paper or presented using a computer package such as Excel. Look at your scattergram.

Describe the pattern shown by your data using the terms 'positive' or 'negative correlation' and 'weak', 'moderate' or 'strong correlation' or 'no correlation'.

_____

_____

Look it up ...

You may want to remind yourself of how these correlations look. Refer to the research methods section of your A2 Student Book.

Step 7 *Inferential statistics and testing for significance*

When you collect data, it is often difficult to see whether the data support your experimental hypothesis. In order to test this formally, psychologists carry out statistical tests to show the likelihood that the result obtained is real (significant) or could have occurred purely by chance.

Choose your statistical test using a number of types of information:

- Did the research look for a difference between sets of scores or a correlation/relationship?
- What type of data was collected?
- If your research looked for a difference, what experimental design was used? Remember that there are different tests for repeated measures and independent groups.

Here, you have carried out a correlational piece of research, so the statistical test you will use is Spearman's rank order correlation coefficient.

Start by putting your data into a table like the one below.

Participant	2D:4DR	Rank	Writing score	Rank	d	D^2
1	1.045	4	3.82	2	−2	4
2	0.951	2	4.73	3	1	1
3	1.035	3	4.83	4	1	1
4	0.943	1	2.38	1	0	0

- Rank the 2D:4DR scores giving the lowest a score of 1 and the highest a score of 10 (or however many participants you had). If you have tied scores, you should give them a tied rank (see the Appendix).
- Repeat this process for the handwriting scores.
- Find the difference (d) between the ranks given to the 2D:4DR score and the rank given to the handwriting score. If the 2D:4DR score is ranked 1 and the writing score is ranked 4, the *d* score would be −3.

- Square this difference, which will get rid of any negative scores.
- Add up the final column to calculate the sum (total) of the d^2 scores.
- Put your data into the formula below:

$$r_s = 1 - \frac{6\Sigma d^2}{N(N^2 - 1)}$$

Work out the formula:

- Multiply (times) the total from the last column of your table (Σd^2) by 6.
- Take the number of participants in your sample (N) and multiply this by itself to find N^2. (If you had 15 participants $15 \times 15 = 225$)
- Multiply the number of participants in your sample by the squared value minus 1 (in the case of 15 participants, this would be 15×224) to find $N(N^2 - 1)$
- Take your answer for $6\Sigma d^2$ and divide this figure by $N(N^2 - 1)$
- Subtract the number from the previous step from 1.

You should now have a number between −1 and +1. A larger number (closer to +1 or −1) indicates a strong relationship, whereas a figure that is close to zero indicates a weak relationship.

- If the number is positive, this indicates a positive correlation.
- If the number is negative, this indicates a negative correlation.

> *This final number is your observed value of Spearman's rho. Write it here.*
>
> _____

Step 8 *Interpret your results. Is the result statistically significant?*

Assess whether the relationship you have found is statistically significant or could have occurred by chance. Compare your observed value with the critical value taken from the table in the Appendix.

- Decide where to look in the table by finding N. N refers to the number of participants used in your study.
- Check whether you had a directional or non-directional hypothesis (and so used one- or a two-tailed test).
- Find the column for a probability level of 0.05.
- The point in the table where these intersect is known as your critical value.
- If your result is equal to or larger than the critical value, you can reject the null hypothesis and accept the alternative hypothesis. You have found a significant correlation.
- If your result is smaller than the critical value, you must retain the null hypothesis. Your data suggest that there is no relationship between the handwriting style of your participants and their finger ratio.
- Complete the statistical conclusion below.

> The observed value of r_s = _____
>
> This was _____ than the critical value of _____
>
> for **N** = _____ probability equal to 0.05
>
> Therefore the null hypothesis was _____

Critical discussion

Theory

- Did your findings support those of Beech and Mackintosh?
- If you retained the null hypothesis, can you think of reasons why this might be?

Methodology

- How reliable were your measurements of 2D:4DR? If you were to repeat the study, how would you measure digit ratio?
- Did you have an appropriate number of judges?
- Were the writing samples sufficiently long to show a real representation of handwriting?
- Was the 5-point rating scale useful or could it have been improved?
- Were your standardised instructions clear?
- When participants are asked to write something special for an experiment, the writing they produce may not be characteristic of their everyday writing. What would be the advantages and drawbacks of using real samples of writing?

Ethics

- Did your study throw up any unseen ethical issues?
- How did your participants feel about taking part?
- What have you learned about research with people?

References

Beech, J.R. and Mackintosh, I.C. (2005) Do differences in sex hormones affect handwriting style? Evidence from digit ratio and sex role identity as determinants of the sex of handwriting. *Personality and Individual Differences*, **39**(2), 459–68.

Rammsayer, T.H. and Troche, S.J. (2007) Sexual dimorphism in 2nd to 4th digit ratio and its relation to gender orientation in males and females. *Personality and Individual Differences*, **42**(6), 911–20.

Young, W.C. (1964) Hormones and sexual behaviour. *Science*, **143**, 212–18.

Intelligence

7 | Gender stereotyping in the perception of intelligence

Learning outcomes for this practical

- A1, A2, A4, A5, B1, B2, B3, B4, C3, D2, E1, E5

Hint

Check these learning outcomes against the list on page iv.

Background

Psychological research shows that there is no significant difference in the levels of general intelligence for men and women. However, since the 1970s a large number of studies have shown that males and females have a different perception of both their own intelligence and of the intelligence of other males and females. If males and females are asked to give estimates of their intelligence, males tend to rate their own intelligence higher than females rate theirs. The higher estimates of male intelligence are not confined to estimates of self-intelligence but also occur in estimates of the intelligence of other males and females. If participants are asked to estimate the intelligence of their mothers and fathers, both males and females are more likely to report that their father is more intelligent than their mother. This gender bias extends to other relatives such as grandmother or grandfather, brother or sister, and so on. The findings have been replicated in many cultures across Europe, Asia, Africa and America. It has been termed the 'male hubris and female humility effect'.

However, this effect seems limited to psychometric intelligence or IQ. When different aspects of intelligence are investigated there are variations between the genders. For example, when asked to estimate levels of the different types of intelligence identified by Gardner (2006), males consistently rated their own mathematical, logical and spatial intelligence higher than females rated theirs. However, females estimated higher scores for themselves than males for musical and interpersonal intelligence. One type of intelligence that seems to be consistently rated as high in females is emotional intelligence (EI). Females tend to estimate that they have higher levels of EI than males. Both males and females tend to estimate that their mothers have a greater emotional intelligence than their fathers. This practical involves testing whether perception of different types of intelligence is associated with different genders.

Look it up

Psychometric intelligence (IQ), and emotional intelligence (EI) are very different ways of describing human intelligence. Revise the concepts of IQ and EI and consider why there might be some gender stereotyping.

Key study

Estimates of emotional and psychometric intelligence: evidence for gender-based stereotypes. (Petrides, Furnham and Martin, 2004)

Participants were asked to estimate their own and their parents' emotional intelligence (EI) and psychometric intelligence (IQ). The 82 male and 158 female participants were asked to estimate both EI and IQ on a scale from 55 (very low) to 145 (very high) points. Both scales showed 100 as being the average score.

When asked to estimate their own levels of intelligence, there were differences between the male and female participants. Males tended to estimate their IQ at a higher level than females. However, the females estimated their EI at a higher level than the males.

Mean estimates of self		
	Males	**Females**
IQ	108.9	105.4
EI	106.6	111.2

The estimates of parental IQ and EI followed this gender bias. When asked to estimate intelligence levels in parents, both males and females tended to rate their fathers as having a higher IQ than their mothers, but they tended to rate their mothers as having a higher EI than their fathers.

Mean estimates of parents		
	Fathers	**Mothers**
IQ	109.7	106.3
EI	99.9	111.7

This table shows that the average estimates of fathers' IQ were slightly higher than mothers' IQ (3.5 points) but that the average estimates of mothers' EI were much higher than fathers' EI (11.8 points). Interestingly, the only estimate that is below the average of 100 is the estimate of fathers' EI.

Method

Step 1 *Design your study: variables and hypotheses*

The first step of the research process is to identify a topic of interest and choose a suitable method to investigate it. Here, the topic of interest is studying whether the perceptions of different types of intelligence are associated with gender.

In a study of association, the researcher does not manipulate an independent variable but investigates whether there is an association between two variables (i.e. whether a difference in one variable is associated with a difference in the other) or whether the two variables are independent (i.e. they do not affect each other). The two variables being investigated in this study are:

- estimates of different types of intelligence
- gender of person being estimated.

In this study we will use a similar method to Petrides *et al.* (2004) and will ask participants to give estimates of IQ and EI for their father and mother. The second variable, gender, represents a categorical variable. These are variables that can only be placed in one category or another (such as male or female). These types of variables generate nominal data. The first variable, estimates of IQ levels, does not initially yield categorical data (i.e. they do not fit into one or the other category). They need to be converted to this kind of data by comparing the scores for mother and father. This is explored in step 3 below.

> **Think about it**
>
> How could estimates of IQ and EI scores for fathers and mothers be converted into categorical data?

Write the hypotheses for your study. The null hypothesis states that the two categorical variables are independent, whereas the experimental hypothesis predicts an association between the two variables. Tests of association between two variables are always two-tailed. It is therefore appropriate to write a non-directional hypothesis.

Write your hypotheses here.

- *Null hypothesis* _____

- *Alternative (experimental) hypothesis* _____

Step 2 *Sampling*

You will need a sample of male and female participants, but you will only need to ask each participant a few questions. As the study is about gender stereotyping of the perception of intelligence, you should try to get a balance of male and female participants. Remember that the participants *must* be over 16. As this is a relatively short procedure, you could select them using one of the following methods:

- a random sample
- an opportunity sample
- a self-selected (volunteer) sample.

Chosen sample method:

_____

> **Ethical issues**
>
> You may wish to look at the section about some of the ethical issues of this study, in Step 4 on page 52, before deciding on a sampling method. Remember that the study will ask participants to estimate both parents' intelligence.

You will also have to think about sample size. For the type of statistical analysis planned for this study, there needs to be a minimum level of participants that are expected in each category. The advice of most statisticians is that you will need to study at least 20 participants to achieve this minimum level.

Step 3 Create instruction sheets and response sheets

Devise a set of standardised instructions for your participants that make it clear exactly what they need to do. You will need to consider carefully what information to include in the instructions. This will depend, in part, on the participants you are likely to have in your sample. In order to get informed responses about parental IQ and EI, participants need to have some understanding of these concepts. If your participants are likely to be fellow psychologists, then a simple reminder may suffice. However, if your participants are non-psychologists you may have to explain in a little more detail what IQ and EI represent.

There are a number of ways to ask participants to estimate the IQ and EI of their father and mother. One is to use a similar method to previous researchers and ask participants to estimate their father's and mother's IQ by marking it on a scale. In common with previous scales, this could range from 55 to 145 and have 100 clearly marked as the average IQ score. Each participant would then be asked to do the same for a scale of EQ. The problem with this method is that many participants may record their father and mother as being the same on either the IQ or EI scale or both. However, the analysis for this study eventually requires nominal data where we record whether the father or mother is estimated to have higher IQ and EI. For this reason, it might be better to give participants simple forced choice questions that ask which parent has the highest IQ and which has highest EI. You could also do this by asking participants to give an IQ and EI estimate rating, but telling them that they cannot give the same value for their mother and father on either scale, again forcing them to produce data that can be made categorical (one or the other being rated as higher).

> **Think about validity**
>
> How would validity be affected if participants do not understand IQ and EQ in this study?

You should devise a simple response sheet that puts these questions clearly and allows space for participants to answer. You should not record participants' names on the response sheets, but you should ask for other information such as sex. This will allow you to record how many males and how many females took part in the study.

Step 4 Ethical issues

As we noted at the start of this workbook, ethical issues guide practical choices and decisions at all stages of the research process. Think about the ethical issues involved in this piece of research.

- An important principle of research is to ensure that participants are able to give their fully informed consent to take part. You should tell potential participants what is involved in the study, what they will be asked to do and roughly how long it will take. You should put this information onto a consent form which you present to your participants to sign. You can view a sample consent form in the Appendix. The consent form should make it clear to your participants that they are free to withdraw at any time.

- Ensure that your research does not put your participants under stress or make them feel uncomfortable. You should therefore make it clear in the information sheet that you will be asking questions about both of the participant's parents. This allows participants who may be uncomfortable with this (e.g. participants with recent bereavements, participants from a one-parent family) to withdraw.

- You will be asking for participants to reveal potentially sensitive information about their estimates of parental intelligence. It is very important that this information remains completely confidential. Firstly, ensure that participants do not reveal their identity on the response sheets. Secondly, you should destroy the response sheets once the data have been tabulated.

- Ensure participants are fully debriefed at the end of the study. You should thank them, tell them what you expect to find and ask whether they have any questions. This is good ethical practice. You should remember to thank every participant after they have taken part.

Step 5 *Piloting*

A pilot study is the last stage of planning, before real data are collected. It enables you to check that your instructions, procedure and response sheets work well. Think about how and where you will collect your data. The environment you use should be kept the same (as far as is practically possible) for all of the participants. This should be relatively noise- and distraction-free. Make sure that you test people without others around to influence them. Try to ensure that the participants do not discuss their responses with participants who have not yet given their estimates as this could influence their responses.

Carry out a short pilot study, testing three or four people to check that your materials and procedure work smoothly.

> **Ethical issues**
>
> Review how you are selecting your sample of participants. Does your method avoid stressing or embarrassing them?

> *Record any problems or changes that are needed to your procedure/instructions here.*
>
> _____
>
> _____
>
> _____

Analysing your data

Step 6 *Organise and display your data*

You should have a completed response sheet from each of your participants. Go through these and tally how many answers fall into one of four categories: father has highest IQ, mother has highest IQ, father has highest EI, mother has highest EI. The tally represents the frequency of each answer. The frequency that is found should be recorded in the table below. It is vital that you record the frequency (or number of answers) in each category and not a percentage or ratio. If data are converted to percentages or ratios, the statistical test becomes invalid.

	IQ	EI
Father highest		
Mother highest		

Plot the four scores in a bar chart. You will need to think of the clearest way of displaying your data. Remember that we are most interested in the comparison of the IQ of fathers and mothers and the comparison of the EI of fathers and mothers (i.e. *not* the comparison of fathers' IQ and EI and mothers' IQ and EI). The table and the bar chart will give you some indication of whether there is a pattern in the data.

Describe any patterns in the data.

_____

_____

Step 7   *Inferential statistics and testing for significance*

In order to test for significance, psychologists carry out statistical tests to show the likelihood that the relationship, association or difference obtained is real (significant) rather than occurring purely by chance. Choose your statistical test using a number of types of information:

- What level of data was collected – nominal or ordinal?
- Did the research look for a difference between sets of data or a relationship between two variables?
- If an experiment has been carried out, what type of design was used?

Write down the statistical test you will use.

_____

Put your data in the table below.

	IQ	EI	Row totals
Father highest	A	B	
Mother highest	C	D	
Column totals			(Grand total)

The data need to meet a number of criteria before we can use a chi-squared test. One of these is that the data need to be categories that are expressed as frequencies. If you have recorded the number of answers in each of the boxes in the table, this criterion should be met. The second is that the data should be independent. In this case, this means that no answer should appear in more than one box.

- The first stage is to calculate the margin totals of the frequency table. Margin totals are the totals for each row and the totals for each column.
- The next stage is to calculate the grand total. This can be found by adding the row totals or the column totals (but not both!). In fact, the sum of the row totals should be the same as the sum of the column totals, and it is useful to check your addition by comparing the two.

- It is convenient to label each of the four boxes of data to help in the calculation of chi-squared.

Essentially a chi-squared test (χ^2) compares what has been observed in each category (i.e. the figure you put in each box) with what would be expected if there was no association between the variables. In the formula below, O represents the observed frequency and E represents the expected frequency. In statistics, the symbol Σ (called 'sigma') represents 'the sum of'.

$$\chi^2 = \Sigma \frac{(O - E)^2}{E}$$

Work out the formula:

- The first stage is to calculate the E value for each of the boxes, A to D, above. The E value is calculated by using the margin totals. The formula is

$$E = \frac{\text{row total} \times \text{column total}}{\text{grand total}}$$

- For each box you will need to take the O value (i.e. the value in the box) and the E value to calculate

$$\frac{(O - E)^2}{E}$$

- Subtract E from O.
- Square this figure.
- Divide the squared value by E.
- Add the values for each box together to give χ^2.

> *This final number is your observed value of chi-squared. Write it here.*
>
> _____

Step 8 *Interpret your results: is the result statistically significant?*

Assess whether the relationship you have found is statistically significant or could have occurred by chance. Compare your observed value with the critical value taken from the table in the Appendix.

- Decide where to look in the table by finding the appropriate degrees of freedom (*df*). The *df* value is linked to the number of categories we have used (how many boxes there were in the original table).

$$df = (\text{Number of rows} - 1) \times (\text{Number of columns} - 1)$$

- For chi-squared all 2-by-2 analyses lead to a two-tailed test.
- Find the column for the probability level of 0.05
- The point in the table where these intersect is known as your critical value.
- If your result is equal to or larger than the critical value, you can reject the null hypothesis and accept the alternative hypothesis. You have found a significant association.

■ If your result is smaller than the critical value, you must retain the null hypothesis. Your data suggest there is no association between perceptions of intelligence and gender.

■ Complete the statistical conclusion below.

The observed value of χ^2 = _____

This was _____ than the critical value of _____

for **df** = _____ probability equal to 0.05

Therefore the null hypothesis was _____

Think about validity

Could the answers that the participants gave be influenced by demand characteristics? Think what you have learned about gender stereotyping and conformity.

This research on a potentially sensitive issue meant the participants needed to be self-selected. How does this affect validity?

Critical discussion

Theory

■ Did your findings support the 'male hubris and female humility effect'? Was there a significant association between perceptions of intelligence and gender?

■ If you retained the null hypothesis, can you think of reasons why this might be?

■ Do you think that gender stereotyping of IQ and EI is as strong now as it was in the 1970s and 1980s?

Methodology

■ Were your standardised instructions clear?

■ Did your participants understand the concepts of IQ and EI?

■ Were the forced choice questions an appropriate way of comparing perceptions of parental intelligence?

■ Was your sample large enough for the chi-squared analysis? Chi-square is prone to Type 1 errors when expected frequencies are low. The general rule of thumb is that the E values should not be less than 5. However, many statisticians suggest that one value can be as low as 2 provided the sample size is 20 or more.

Ethics

■ Did your study throw up any unseen ethical issues?

■ How did your participants feel about taking part?

■ What have you learned about research with people?

References

Gardner, H. (2006) *Multiple intelligences: New Horizons*. New York: Basic Books.

Petrides, K.V., Furnham, A. and Martin, G.N. (2004) Estimates of emotional and psychometric intelligence: Evidence for gender-based stereotypes. *The Journal of Social Psychology*, **144**, 149–62.

Cognition and development

8 Is there an association between gender and moral reasoning?

Learning outcomes for this practical

- A1, A2, A4, A5, B1, B3, B4, C1, C2, C5, D2, E1, E5

Hint

Check these learning outcomes against the list on page iv.

Background

How do young people develop ideas about right and wrong? There is wide agreement that children develop moral understanding in a series of stages that are loosely linked to age. Much of the early research into moral development was carried out by Laurence Kohlberg using moral judgement interviews (MJIs). In these interviews, Kohlberg presented his participants with a series of moral 'dilemmas' such as the one shown below. Using questions like those shown, they were asked to comment on the actions taken by the characters in the drama and to explain whether the behaviours were morally acceptable or morally wrong.

Example of a moral dilemma used by Kohlberg

Two young men, brothers, had got into serious trouble. They were secretly leaving town in a hurry and needed money. Karl, the older one, broke into a store and stole a thousand dollars. Bob, the younger one, went to a retired old man who was known to help people in town. He told the man that he was very sick and that he needed a thousand dollars to pay for an operation. Bob asked the old man to lend him the money and promised that he would pay him back when he recovered. Really Bob wasn't sick at all, and he had no intention of paying the man back. Although the old man didn't know Bob very well, he lent him the money. So Bob and Karl skipped town, each with a thousand dollars.

1a Which is worse, stealing like Karl or cheating like Bob?

1b Why is that worse?

In 1963, Kohlberg carried out a series of research studies with American boys aged between 7 and 16 to investigate the development of moral reasoning. From these studies, he devised a model of moral reasoning with three 'levels', each subdivided into two stages. In Level 1, children judge right and wrong on the basis of reward or punishment. Behaviour that leads to punishment is seen as wrong, and behaviour that leads to reward is seen as right (the pre-conventional level). At Level 2, children internalise the rules of the family and wider society and use these to decide on right and wrong (the conventional level). At Level 3, individuals make their own moral judgements according to their own set of values (post-conventional morality). Kohlberg found that the last level was only reached by some adults, with many people remaining at Level 2.

In later studies, Kohlberg tested girls and women using the same set of moral dilemmas that were used in his original study. He found that girls and women achieved a lower level of moral understanding in his model than men and boys, which led him to conclude that females were less morally developed than males. This view was criticised by Carol Gilligan, one of Kohlberg's students. Gilligan argued that Kohlberg's model was gender biased as it had been developed entirely from research using males. Gilligan carried out research into moral reasoning in women using different kinds of moral problems to those used by Kohlberg.

Key study

Moral reasoning in women (Gilligan, 1994)

Gilligan interviewed 29 American women aged between 15 and 33 who were presented with a real-life moral decision faced by many women each year. This decision focused on whether to continue with an unwanted pregnancy or to have an abortion. Gilligan found that women produced three kinds of moral reasoning, and she divided these into three different levels:

- Level 1 Self interest: at this level, women referred solely to their own needs and interests in their decision about the pregnancy. For example, they might justify ending a pregnancy because their career would be damaged.

- Level 2 Self sacrifice: at this level, women referred to the needs and feelings of people around them, such as their partner or parents. They might decide to continue with a pregnancy because their partner wanted a child, or end the pregnancy because their parents put them under pressure to do so.

- Level 3 Care as a universal obligation: at this level, women tried to balance the demands and feelings of other people and their own choices, needs and well-being. Their decision regarding the pregnancy took the feelings and needs of many people into account.

Gilligan argued that men and women think differently about right and wrong. She argued that men reason on the basis of justice or doing what is *fair*. In contrast, women reason on the basis of *care*, taking into account other people's feelings. Their moral reasoning is oriented towards looking after those who are in need.

As you can see, there is a debate here regarding sex differences in moral reasoning. While Kohlberg argued that men achieve a higher level of moral reasoning, Gilligan has argued that women think differently to men about moral issues. Despite these claims, many studies have found no differences in moral reasoning between men and women. A meta-review of 41 studies of gender differences in moral reasoning indicated that 85 per cent found no differences at all (Walker, 1984). Your task is to re-examine this debate by comparing the moral judgements made by male and female participants using a moral dilemma similar to Kohlberg's.

Before you design your study, a word about ethics

This piece of practical work involves ethical issues, which must be considered before you plan the nuts and bolts of data collection.

There are many moral dilemmas in evidence in everyday life. For example, newspapers often report cases involving 'mercy killings' in which a relative or doctor has assisted the suicide of a terminally ill person at their request, risking possible prosecution. A related debate considers whether it is morally acceptable to end someone's life when they have reached a permanent vegetative state (i.e. they are brain dead) after an accident.

At the time of writing, it is acceptable within British law to allow someone to die by withdrawing feeding, but it is against the law to end someone's life by taking positive action to do so. Real-life examples of this nature are extremely sensitive. These cases – while directly relevant to moral reasoning – generate strong feelings and may also lead to unpleasant emotions of stress and anxiety in participants. For this reason, rather than use an issue such as this we have provided you with a moral dilemma similar to those used by Kohlberg. The following dilemma should enable you to examine moral reasoning without causing undue stress to the participants.

> Two girls, both teenagers, wanted to go to a music festival but did not have £170.00 to buy weekend tickets. Katy stole the money over several weeks by overcharging people a small amount in the paper shop where she worked. Tina visited her elderly grandmother and told her that she needed to borrow some money to buy a birthday present for her mother. She told her grandmother that she would return the money by getting a part-time job and saving up. In fact, Tina had no intention of paying her grandmother back. Both girls managed to buy their tickets and went to the festival.
>
> 1 Which is worse, stealing like Katy or cheating and lying like Tina?
>
> 2 Why is that worse?

Method

Step 1 Identify and operationalise variables

In a study of association, the researcher does not manipulate an independent variable but investigates whether there is an association between two variables (i.e. whether a change in one variable is associated with a change in the other) or whether the two variables are independent (i.e. they do not affect each other). The two variables investigated in this study are:

- the sex of the participant – male or female
- the type of moral reasoning – based on justice or based on care.

These two variables are categorical as participants are placed in one of the two categories noted above. This method is relevant to the study as the variable we are interested in, the sex of participants, cannot be manipulated and occurs naturally. In order to measure the sex of your participants, simply ask them to record it on their written response using a tick box.

The second variable in this study is moral reasoning/judgement measured using the dilemma described above. The participants will be asked to provide a written response in which they identify whose behaviour is morally worse and then explain why they have made this judgement. These data are qualitative as they are non-numeric. In order to convert the data into quantitative format for statistical

Look it up …

You may want to refresh your memory about qualitative data by looking back at the relevant section in your A2 Student Book.

analysis, you will need to categorise each response into one category only – justice or care. There are various ways of doing this and we will explore these in step 5 (piloting).

Step 2 *Hypotheses*

Write the hypotheses for your study. The null hypothesis states that the two categorical variables are independent and that there will be no association between them. The experimental hypothesis predicts that there will be an association between the two variables. Tests of association between two variables are always two-tailed as they indicate whether an association exists but not exactly what it is. It is therefore appropriate to write a non-directional hypothesis for this practical or for any exercise in which chi-squared test is used to analyse the data.

Write your hypotheses here.

■ *Null hypothesis* _____

■ *Non-directional* _____

Step 3 *Ethical issues*

Ethical issues guide practical choices and decisions at all stages of the research process. Think about the ethical issues involved in this piece of research.

■ An important principle of research is to enable participants to give their fully informed consent to take part. This is particularly important when the nature of the topic is sensitive: many people have very strong ideas about right and wrong and these may be linked to religious beliefs. Ensure that potential participants are given very clear information about the nature of the study before agreeing to take part. In this case, before they give their consent show your participants the dilemma they will be asked to discuss. Put this information onto a consent form and ask them to sign it. You can see a sample consent form in the Appendix on page 92. The consent form should make it clear to your participants that they are free to withdraw at any time.

■ Ensure that your research does not put your participants under stress or make them feel uncomfortable. If you ask them questions about their answers/ moral judgements, they may feel that they have to justify their views. For this reason, ask participants to complete their response to the dilemma in private and to put this into a box, so they cannot be identified or linked with the data.

■ You will be asking participants to reveal potentially sensitive information about their moral beliefs. It is very important that this information remains completely confidential. Firstly, ensure that participants do not reveal their identity on the response sheets. Secondly, destroy the response sheets once the data have been tabulated.

■ Ensure participants are fully debriefed at the end of the study. Tell them what you expect to find and ask whether they have any questions. This is good ethical practice. Remember to thank every participant after they have taken part.

Step 4   *Sampling*

You will need a sample of male and female participants. Your participants *must* be over 16. Because age may affect moral reasoning, you should also ensure that the participants are of a similar age in order to prevent age acting as a confounding variable.

As this is a relatively short procedure, you could select the participants using one of the following methods:

- a random sample
- an opportunity sample
- a self-selected (volunteer) sample.

Chosen sample method:

_____

You will also have to think about sample size. For the type of statistical analysis planned for this study, there needs to be a minimum level of participants expected in each category. The advice of most statisticians is that you will need to study at least 20 participants to achieve this minimum level. As the study is about gender differences, try to get a balance of male and female participants. It is fine to collect more data than this.

Step 5   *Create instruction sheets and response sheets*

Devise a data sheet that gives your participants clear instructions to follow. This sheet should have the dilemma clearly printed at the top, followed by the two questions with spaces for participants to write their answers. You will need to encourage your participants to think carefully about the dilemma and to opt for a clear answer rather than sitting on the fence. Do not ask your participants to record their names on the response sheet, but you must ask them to identify whether they are male or female as this is crucial to your study.

Step 6   *Piloting*

A pilot study is the last stage of planning, before real data are collected. It enables you to check that your instructions, procedures and response sheets work well. In this practical it is also vital in helping you to decide how you will code your data. Think about how and where you will collect your data. The environment you use should be kept the same (as far as is practically possible) for all of the participants. This should be relatively noise- and distraction-free. Make sure that you test people without others around to influence them. Age may also be an extraneous variable and you only want to be measuring the difference that the participants' sex makes, so try to aim for participants of a similar age.

> **Hint**
>
> Coding is a specific way of choosing to categorise data.

Record any problems or changes needed to your procedure/instructions here.

_____

_____

_____

_____

When you have collected three or four pieces of data, think about how you will categorise the responses. Remember that you need to categorise each response into *one* category only – justice or care.

The simplest system is to categorise responses using the answer to question 1 only. If a participant responds by arguing that Katy is morally worse because her behaviour breaks the law, they should be classed in the category of 'justice'. If they argue that Tina is morally worse as her behaviour breaks moral rules, they should be placed into the category of 'care'.

A more complicated method is to read through each response and count the number of references made to the law (justice) or to other people's feelings (care) in the answers to question 2. Using this method, the larger number of references should determine which category the response is placed in. You may also think of other methods as you look at your data. Try out these approaches using your pilot data and decide which you will use. Record this below.

> **Think about it**
>
> Consider how different ways of categorising your data would affect the reliability and validity of your study.

I will code the data by: _____

_____

Analysing your data

Step 7 *Organise and display your data*

You should have a completed response sheet from each of the participants. Go through these and use your chosen coding system to tally how many answers fall into each of the four categories in the table below. The tally represents the frequency of each answer. It is important that you record the frequency (or number of answers) in each category and not a percentage or ratio. If data are converted to percentages or ratios, the statistical test becomes invalid.

	Male	Female
Reasoning based on justice		
Reasoning based on care		

Display your data by plotting the four scores in a bar chart. The table and the bar chart will give you some indication of whether there is a pattern in the data.

> *Describe any patterns in the data.*
>
> _____
>
> _____

Step 8 *Inferential statistics and testing for significance*

In order to test for significance, psychologists carry out statistical tests to show the likelihood that the relationship, association or difference obtained is real (significant) rather than occurring purely by chance. Choose your statistical test using a number of types of information:

- What level of data was collected – nominal or ordinal?
- Did the research look for a difference between sets of data or a relationship between two variables?
- If an experiment has been carried out, what type of design was used?

> *Write down the statistical test you will use.*
>
> _____

Look it up …

You can refresh your memory about test choice using the flow chart in the Appendix on page 91.

The data need to meet a number of criteria before we can use a chi-squared test. One of these is that the data need to be in categories expressed as frequencies. If you have recorded the number of answers in each of the boxes in the table, this criterion should be met. The second criterion is that data should be independent. In this case, this means that no answer should appear in more than one box.

	Male	Female	Row totals
Justice	A	B	
Care	C	D	
Column totals			(Grand total)

- The first stage is to calculate the margin totals of the frequency table. Margin totals are the totals of each row and the totals of each column.
- The next stage is to calculate the grand total. This can be found by adding the row totals or the column totals (but not both!). In fact, the sum of the row totals should be the same as the sum of the column totals and it is useful to check your addition by comparing the two.
- It is convenient to label each of the four boxes of data to help in the calculation of chi-squared. In the above example, the boxes (or cells) are labelled A to D.

Essentially a chi-squared test (χ^2) compares what has been observed in each category (i.e. the figure you put in each box) with what would be expected if there was no association between the variables. In the formula below, O represents the observed frequency and E represents the expected frequency. In statistics, the symbol Σ (sigma) means 'the sum of'.

$$\chi^2 = \Sigma \frac{(O-E)^2}{E}$$

Work out the formula:

■ The first stage is to calculate the E value for each of the boxes, A to D, above. The E value is calculated by using the margin totals. The formula is:

$$E = \frac{\text{row total} \times \text{column total}}{\text{grand total}}$$

■ For each box you will need to take the O value (i.e. the value in the box) and the E value to calculate

$$\frac{(O-E)^2}{E}$$

■ The first stage is to subtract E from O.
■ Square this figure.
■ Divide the squared value by E.
■ Add the values for each box together to give χ^2.

> *This final number is your observed value of chi-squared. Write it here.*
>
> _____

Step 9 *Interpret your results. Is the result statistically significant?*

Assess whether the relationship you have found is statistically significant or could have occurred by chance. Compare your observed value with the critical value taken from the table in the Appendix.

■ Decide where to look in the table by finding the appropriate degrees of freedom (*df*). The *df* value is linked to the number of categories we have used (how many boxes there were in the original table).

$$df = (\text{Number of rows} - 1) \times (\text{Number of columns} - 1)$$

■ For chi-squared, all 2-by-2 analyses lead to a two-tailed test.
■ Find the column for probability level of 0.05.
■ The point in the table where these intersect is known as your critical value.
■ If your result is equal to or larger than the critical value, you can reject the null hypothesis and accept the alternative hypothesis. You have found a significant association.
■ If your result is smaller than the critical value, you must retain the null hypothesis. Your data suggest there is no association between sex and moral reasoning.
■ Complete the statistical conclusion below.

The observed value of χ^2 = _____

This was _____ than the critical value of _____

for **df** = _____ probability equal to 0.05

Therefore the null hypothesis was _____

Critical discussion

Theory

- Did you find a difference in moral reasoning between males and females?
- If so, was this consistent with Gilligan's claim that men reason on the basis of justice and women on the basis of care?
- If you found no difference, why do you think this might be?

Methodology

- Here we used one moral dilemma, but Kohlberg used several in his moral judgement interviews. How might this have influenced your findings?
- Did your participants understand what they were asked to do?
- How useful were the forced choice questions in eliciting moral judgements? Did they have limitations?
- Was your sample large enough for the chi-squared analysis? Chi-squared is prone to Type 1 errors when expected frequencies are low. The general rule of thumb is that the E values should not be less than 5. However, many statisticians suggest that one value can be as low as 2 provided the sample size is 20 or more.

Ethics

- Did your study throw up any ethical issues?
- How did your participants feel about taking part?
- What have you learned about research with people?

References

Gilligan, C. (1994) In a different voice: Women's conception of self and morality. In B. Puka (ed.) *Caring Voices and Women's Moral Frames: Gilligan's View*. New York: Garland Publishing.

Kohlberg, L. (1963) The development of children's orientations toward a moral order: I. *Sequence in the development of moral thought*. Human Development, **6**, 11–33.

Walker, L.J. (1984) Sex differences in the development of moral reasoning: A critical review. *Child Development*, **55**, 677–91.

Media psychology

9 Content analysis of TV election broadcasts

Learning outcomes for this practical

- A1, A2, A5, B1, B2, B4, C4, D2, E1, E5

Hint

Check these learning outcomes against the list on page iv.

Background

How easily are people persuaded by material shown on television? The Hovland-Yale model of attitude change suggested that persuasion took place in four stages: attention, comprehension, reactance and finally attitude change. Many studies have investigated factors that influence persuasion. These have been classified loosely as the source (*who* is presenting the argument) the message (*what* is being said) and the recipient (the *target* of the message). Evidence suggests that sources are most persuasive when they appear to be knowledgeable/expert and when they are attractive. Messages are generally more persuasive when they are repeated. Many studies have pointed to the important role played by fear in persuasion and attitude change.

How do these findings translate to election campaigns? Television has been an extremely influential medium in election campaigns since the 1960s. Television broadcasts enable political parties to present favourable messages about their policies and achievements to persuade the electorate to vote for them. They also provide an opportunity to comment critically on the policies, achievements and personalities of their political opponents. In recent years, televised debates between political leaders have become a feature of election campaigns in the US and the UK. The development of internet sites such as YouTube means that broadcasts and debates remain in the public arena so they can be rewatched at will. Election campaign posters provide a rich ground for comedians and satirists. (See 'Airbrushed for change' posters of the 2010 election, which you can find on various websites.) Material of this nature provides a rich and highly valid source of data for studying the processes involved in successful election campaigns.

Look it up ...

You can look up these studies on persuasion in your A2 Student Book. Content analysis is a quantitative method in which the content of books, newspapers or TV programmes is examined and features are counted to see how often they occur. You can refresh your memory of this method by looking back at the research methods section of your A2 Student Book.

Key study

Hacker and Swan (1992)

How do politicians persuade people to vote for them? Hacker and Swan used content analysis to examine the television broadcasts produced by two political parties in the 1988 American election in which the Republican candidate, George H. Bush defeated the Democrat, Michael Dukakis. The aim of their study was to examine the messages used by each side in the election campaign. Hacker and Swan videotaped 17 campaign broadcasts and then randomly selected five from each candidate for analysis. They watched and re-watched the broadcasts many times in order to devise a coding system. They divided each broadcast into a number of sections, which they called clips. Then they watched each of the clips again and classified each separate section within them into categories based on the type of content. Some of the categories they used were:

Positive record: References to a past positive achievements of a candidate.

Negative record: References to past negative events, usually of their opponent.

Positive traits: References to positive personal qualities of the candidate.

Negative traits: References to negative personal qualities of the candidate or their opponent.

Family: A message that showed the candidate with their own family or with other families/children.

Vision statements: A message that portrayed the candidate's vision for the future, such as a slogan like' Things can only get better' or 'The Big Society'.

Fear: A message designed to make the watcher afraid of what the other party would do if they were elected.

Using this system, each clip was classified for the medium of the message (verbal/pictorial etc.) as well as the content of the message.

When the researchers compared the two campaigns, they found that Bush, the eventual winner, used significantly more references to his own positive traits and positive past records than Dukakis, the loser. In contrast, Dukakis used significantly more vision statements than Bush. Other minor differences, which were not significant, included reference in Dukakis's material to George Bush's negative traits.

Hacker and Swan's study demonstrates many important aspects of persuasive messages. It also shows how the analysis of real materials can contribute to our understanding of persuasion and allow us to see whether theories/models derived from laboratory studies apply in the real world.

> **Hint**
>
> What Hacker and Swan refer to as 'clips' are the segments of the broadcast that give one particular message and can be called 'message units'.

Your task is to use the same method as Hacker and Swan – content analysis – to compare the messages put forward by *two* party leaders in election broadcasts. We will concentrate on spoken statements and visual images in televised broadcasts. Choose a national election that has taken place recently, but you can focus on any country that you are familiar with. The two people you choose to study should include the eventual winner of the election and a leader of a key opposition party who lost the election. The most important criterion in making your choice is that internet coverage of the broadcasts is freely available for you to use for data collection.

> **Hint**
>
> This practical works best when you are able to work in pairs or groups. This enables checks for inter-rater reliability to be carried out.

Method

Step 1 *Variables and hypotheses*

In a study of association, the researcher does not manipulate an independent variable but investigates whether there is an association between two variables (i.e. whether a change in one variable is associated with a change in the other) or whether the two variables are independent (i.e. they do not affect each other). In this piece of research, we are looking to see whether there is an association between the content of election broadcasts and the outcome of the election. The two variables investigated are therefore:

- the outcome of the election: whether the candidate won or lost
- the content of the broadcast message, particularly the number of positive and negative references.

These two variables are categorical as the messages in the broadcasts are placed into categories. In this content analysis, each message unit is placed in one of the four cells (see the table in step 6 on page 70). Tests of association between two variables are always two-tailed as they indicate whether an association exists but not exactly what it is. It is therefore appropriate to write a non-directional hypothesis for this practical or for any exercise in which a chi-squared test is used to analyse the data.

Write the hypotheses for your study.

> *Write your hypotheses here.*
>
> - *Null hypothesis* _____
>
> - *Non-directional hypothesis* _____

Step 2 *Sampling*

Find out what material is available on the internet for you to analyse. You will need to spend a reasonable amount of time searching internet sites for coverage of your chosen election and you should identify at least 10 broadcasts (Hacker and Swan were able to locate 17 of the American election, but you may find more). These should be television *or* web broadcasts and they are likely to be around 2–3 minutes long. Ensure that each broadbcast is selected once only and remember that the same one may appear on several websites. The number of available broadcasts will form the target population from which you will select your sample for content analysis.

Choose your sample of broadcasts to analyse. Aim for between two and five for each candidate. An easy method of selecting a random sample would be to give each broadcast a number and use the random number function on a calculator to select which to analyse. To choose a systematic sample, you could make an alphabetical list and then select every third (or fifth) on the list. Whichever method you decide to use, you should ensure that your broadcasts are chosen in an unbiased way.

Record your sampling decisions below.

General election country and date: _____

Candidates chosen for analysis: _____

_____

Number of broadcasts identified in total: _____

Method of choosing sample broadcasts: _____

_____

_____

Step 3 *Ethical issues*

In this piece of practical work, you will be dealing with material that is in the public arena and is freely available for you to view over the internet. Under these conditions, it is impossible for you to ask for informed consent to study the broadcasts. When material has been placed in the public arena, it is reasonable to assume that consent has been given for it to be viewed and discussed.

Step 4 *Piloting and inter-rater reliability*

Piloting is often the most time-consuming aspect of practical work. In content analysis, more time is likely to be spent piloting than analysing your real data. Select two broadcasts for pilot study purposes. Choose one of these and work with one other person. In common with Hacker and Swan, divide each one into clips or message units. These are sections of the broadcast that deal with a particular message. They can be visual (a scene from a broadcast) or oral (spoken statements about a candidate or policy). Discuss each message unit and decide as a pair which of the categories below it fits into. You may find that there are lots of arguments at this stage as you are working out exactly what the categories mean. You may also find that several of the message units are classed as 'other'. Each message unit should be given a brief label or description from the coding system used below.

> **Think about validity**
>
> In many kinds of qualitative research, the coding system is developed *from* the data. The researcher looks at the data with an open mind to see the types of categories to use rather than deciding them beforehand. Here, we will code the data using categories from the framework put forward by Hacker and Swan so that we can compare our findings to theirs.

Type of reference	Code
Positive record	PR
Negative record	NR
Positive trait	PT
Negative trait	NT
Family	FA
Fear	FE
Other	O

When you have worked your way through the first pilot broadcast, you and your partner should code the other one separately from each other with no discussion. After you have done this, get back together and compare your answers. You should be in rough agreement about the number of message units. You should aim to agree on about 80 per cent of the labels you have assigned. If you agree on that number of labels, you can continue with your main data collection. If you agree on less than that, you will need to discuss the message units that have led to disagreement and decide how they will be categorised.

Hint

You and your partner may have trouble agreeing on the message units after your first attempt at coding them. If that happens, in order to progress you could work together to decide the message unit boundaries for all of the media you are covering and then split up to code the various message types.

Step 5 Data collection

Now you can go ahead and categorise the remainder of the broadcasts in your sample. You may find that you need to watch each one several times and to pause the broadcast in order to record your findings. Record your data for each candidate using a tally table similar to the one below.

Candidate – Election winner _____		Statements	Visual images	Total
Positive references	Positive record (PR)	III	II	5
	Positive trait (PT)	IIII		4
	Family (FA)	III	IIII	7
Negative references	Negative record (NR)		II	2
	Negative trait (NT)	I		I
	Fear (FE)	II	IIII	6
	Other (O)	IIIIII	III	9

Analysing your data

Step 6 Organise and display your data

You should now have two completed tables, one for each politician. You will need to calculate the total positive references and the total negative references made in the broadcasts. Put these into a table like the one below.

Candidate	Election winner (_____)	Election loser (_____)
Number of positive references		
Number of negative references		

It is vital that you record the number (or frequency) of references in each category and not a percentage or ratio. If data are converted to percentages or ratio, the statistical test you are going to use, chi-squared, becomes invalid. Plot the four scores in a bar chart. You will need to think of the clearest way of displaying your data. Remember that we are most interested in the comparison between the election winner and loser rather than between positive and negative references in general. The table and the bar chart will indicate whether there are differences in the election messages.

Describe any patterns in the data.

_____

_____

_____

_____

Step 7 *Inferential statistics and testing for significance*

In order to test for significance, psychologists carry out statistical tests to show the likelihood that the relationship, association or difference obtained is real (significant) rather than occurring purely by chance. Choose your statistical test using a number of types of information:

■ What level of data was collected – nominal or ordinal?

■ Did the research look for a difference between sets of data or a relationship between two variables?

■ If an experiment has been carried out, what type of design was used?

Write down the statistical test you will use.

_____

The data need to meet a number of criteria before we can use a chi-squared test. One criterion is that the data need to be frequencies, and fit in categories. If you have recorded the number of message units in each of the boxes in the table, this criterion should be met. The second criterion is that the data should be independent. In this case, this means that no answer should appear in more than one box.

	Winner	Loser	Row totals
Positive references	A	B	
Negative references	C	D	
Column totals			(Grand total)

■ The first stage is to calculate the margin totals of the frequency table. Margin totals are the totals for each row and the totals for each column.

■ The next stage is to calculate the grand total. This can be found by adding the row totals or the column totals (but not both). In fact, the sum of the row totals should be the same as the sum of the column totals and it is useful to check your addition by comparing the two.

- It is convenient to label each of the four boxes of data to help in the calculation of chi-squared.

Essentially a chi-squared test (χ^2) compares what has been observed in each category (i.e. the figure you put in each box) with what would be expected if there was no association between the variables. In the formula below, O represents the observed frequency and E represents the expected frequency. In statistics, the symbol Σ (sigma) means 'the sum of'.

$$\chi^2 = \Sigma \frac{(O - E)^2}{E}$$

Work out the formula:

- The first stage is to calculate the E value for each of the boxes, A to D, on page 71. The E value is calculated by using the margin totals. The formula is:

$$E = \frac{\text{row total} \times \text{column total}}{\text{grand total}}$$

- For each box you will need to take the O value (i.e. the value in the box) and the E value to calculate

$$\frac{(O - E)^2}{E}$$

- The first stage is to subtract E from O.
- Square this figure.
- Divide the squared value by E.
- Add the values for each box together to give χ^2.

This final number is your observed value of chi-squared. Write it here.

_____

Step 8 *Interpret your results. Is the result statistically significant?*

Assess whether the relationship you have found is statistically significant or could have occurred by chance. Compare your observed value with the critical value taken from the table in the Appendix.

- Decide where to look in the table by finding the appropriate degrees of freedom (*df*). The *df* value is linked to the number of categories we have used (how many boxes there were in the original table).

$$df = (\text{Number of rows} - 1) \times (\text{Number of columns} - 1)$$

- For chi-squared, all 2-by-2 analyses lead to a two-tailed test.
- Find the column for probability level of 0.05.
- The point in the table where these intersect is known as your critical value.
- If your result is equal to or larger than the critical value, you can reject the null hypothesis and accept the alternative hypothesis. You have found a significant association.

- If your result is smaller than the critical value, you must retain the null hypothesis. Your data suggest there is no association between the content of a message and the outcome of an election.

- Complete the statistical conclusion below.

The observed value of χ^2 = _____

This was _____ than the critical value of _____

for **df** = _____ probability equal to 0.05

Therefore the null hypothesis was _____

Critical discussion

Theory

- Did you find a difference in the types of message put forward by the election winner and loser?

- If so, was this consistent with Hacker and Swan's claim that winners use more references to their own positive traits and achievements?

- If you found no difference, why do you think this might be?

- One criticism of studies of association is that they cannot tell us about cause and effect. In this case, we cannot conclude that the type of broadcast caused a candidate to win or lose an election. What factors may influence the outcome of general elections other than party propaganda?

- What advice might you give to 'spin doctors' about successful election campaigns based on the findings here?

Methodology

- How well did your sampling system work?

- Were the categories used by Hacker and Swan sufficient to categorise the message units shown in your chosen broadcasts?

- Do you think there may be cultural differences between the types of broadcast put together in the US and the country you studied?

- How easy was it to achieve a reliable system of coding the data?

- What are the advantages and disadvantages of using internet broadcasts to investigate media and persuasion?

References

Hacker, K.L. and Swan, W.O. (1992) Content analysis of the Bush and Dukakis 1988 presidential campaign commercials. *Journal of Social Behaviour and Personality*, **7**(3), 367–74.

Addictive behaviour

10 Is there an addictive personality?

> **Learning outcomes for this practical**
> * A1, A2, A4, A5, B1, B3, B4, C1, C2, C3, C5, D2, E2, E5

Hint

Check these learning outcomes against the list on page iv.

Background

One explanation of addictive behaviour focuses on internal factors, with the idea that some kinds of people are more likely to develop addictions than others. There is some support for this view. Deverensky *et al.* (2003) found that adolescent gamblers have a low self-esteem and higher-than-normal rates of depression. Button *et al.* (1997) also found that those with low self-esteem are at greater risk of addictive behaviour and eating disorders. These findings point to the important role played by self-esteem in addictive behaviours.

Another important factor may be personality. In the case of people with drug dependence, Francis (1996) discovered high scores on the neuroticism and psychoticism scales of Eysenck's personality inventory. These findings suggest that some people may be predisposed to developing addictive behaviours, a claim made by personality theorist, Hans Eysenck. Of course, there are problems drawing conclusions about the impact of personality types on addictive behaviour when the research is correlational. Is a person moody, irritable and anxious (the characteristics of neuroticism) because they take drugs, or is this the reason for them taking drugs?

A recently identified addiction is the use of technology such as social networking sites like Facebook or Twitter and mobile phone usage. A growing body of evidence points to the important role played by personality in addictions to various kinds of technology. The aim of this practical is to investigate whether there is a correlation between the amount of mobile phone usage and personality type. There are fewer ethical issues and complications involved in asking people about their phone usage than asking them about gambling habits or drug or alcohol dependence. Questions about the use of mobile phones are less likely to provoke negative reactions in your participants and people are likely to tell the truth.

Phillips and Butt (2008) were interested in examining possible links between mobile phone usage and personality type. In order to study this, they selected 112 owners of mobile phones and asked them to report on their phone usage (e.g. number of texts sent, phone calls made and the number of times they checked their phone per day). Each participant was also asked to complete a personality measurement that examined four dimensions of personality (extroversion, agreeableness, neuroticism and conscientiousness) as well as levels of self-esteem. Extroversion is a personality type that is characterised by

Hint

People can get different results on personality tests on different days. This can be due to different moods or memories of specific experiences that the test questions may evoke for people. It is important to remember that these tests are a snapshot and do not predetermine the rest of the participant's life. So make sure that your participants are aware of the limitations of these tests and do not base their future life decisions on their outcome.

outgoing, sociable behaviour. Extroverts find it hard to spend time on their own. Neuroticism is a personality type in which an individual finds it hard to cope with anxieties and conflicts.

Phillips and Butt found a range of interesting correlations between personality and phone use. There was a positive correlation between overall extroversion and the amount of time spent using a phone for entertainment or stimulation, such as changing ring tones and wallpaper. Those who scored highly on both extroversion and neuroticism were more likely to send greater numbers of SMS (text) messages.

Method

Step 1 *Design your study: variables and hypotheses*

The first step of the research process is to operationalise the variables that you intend to investigate. In a correlational study, the researcher does not manipulate an independent variable but measures two co-variables to establish whether there is a pattern or relationship between them. The two co-variables measured in this correlational study are:

- the amount of daily usage of a mobile phone
- the personality of your participants.

The amount of daily phone usage can be measured by asking your participants to count up how many text messages they have sent over a 24-hour period. Do this by asking them not to delete the messages, so that at the end of the period they can count them and provide you with a total number. Alternatively, if your participants have a previous 24-hours worth of messages for you to count, you could add up how many they have sent.

Research has identified several different personality types, notably extroversion/introversion, that are linked to addictive behaviour. Select a suitable personality test to administer to your participants. There are several to choose from on the website http://xestia.net/tests/index.html. Choose one of these tests, or choose one from another website. Click through it yourself and then pick an appropriate trait (aspect) of personality to measure that you think will be related to mobile phone usage.

Write the hypotheses for your study. The null hypothesis states that there will be no relationship between two variables, whereas the alternative hypothesis predicts there will be a relationship. You will need to decide whether your alternative hypothesis should be directional (use a one-tailed test) or non-directional (use a two-tailed test). Non-directional hypotheses are chosen when there is insufficient research to point to the outcome of the study or when previous research studies have produced conflicting results (you do not know what the outcome will be).

> **Look it up ...**
>
> Refresh your memory about the characteristics of addictive behaviour by looking at your A2 Student Book. Excessive usage of a mobile phone might be justified due to a person's job, for example. What type of behaviour would suggest that high usage is an addiction?

> **Look it up ...**
>
> Refresh your memory about correlational studies and writing hypotheses by looking back at the research methods section in your A2 Student Book.

Write your hypotheses here.

■ *Null hypothesis* _____

■ *Alternative (experimental) hypothesis* _____

Justify your choice of a directional or non-directional hypothesis here.

I have chosen a _____ *hypothesis because* _____

_____

_____

Step 2 *Sampling*

Choosing your participants should be fairly easy. The only criterion is that they must all possess a mobile phone and use it for sending text messages. There are several different sampling techniques that you could use:

- an opportunity sample
- a self-selecting (volunteer) sample
- a stratified sample.

You might want to consider trying to reduce participant variables when you select who to use. One way of doing this would be to only use participants of the same age. This might mean that you just use your friends (opportunity sample) or that you put up an advertisement in the students' common room at your school or college asking for volunteers. Remember that whichever method you use, you *must* make sure that all of your participants are at least 16 years old.

Step 3 *Ethical issues*

Ethical issues guide practical choices and decisions at all stages of the research process. Think about the ethical issues involved in this piece of research.

- An important principle of research is to enable participants to give their fully informed consent to take part, knowing what they will be letting themselves in for. Tell potential participants what is involved in the study, what they will be asked to do and roughly how long it will take. Put this information on a consent form and ask the participants to sign it. You can view a sample consent form in the Appendix on page 92. The consent form should make it clear to your participants that they are free to withdraw at any time.

- Ensure that your research does not put your participants under stress or make them feel uncomfortable. You may find that some participants are reluctant to take a personality test if they think they might discover something unpleasant about themselves. On the other hand, they might be happy to take the test to begin with, but become unhappy afterwards if they realise they have low self-esteem. Be sensitive to this when asking for consent and collecting your data.

> **Think about controls**
>
> Control is an important principle of research design. You need to ensure that the procedure and instructions are standardised as far as possible. How could the day of the week that each participant chooses to record the number of text messages they send be important in this study?

- Maintain confidentiality. Whatever the results of your test are, do not reveal anyone's identity. A good way to ensure confidentiality is to refer to the participants using numbers or letters rather than their names.

- Ensure participants are fully debriefed at the end of the study. Make sure you include some information about not taking the results from the personality tests too seriously (see the Hint box on page 74). Tell them what you expect to find and ask whether they have any questions. This is good ethical practice. Remember to thank every participant after they have taken part.

Step 4 *Piloting*

A pilot study is the last stage of planning before real data are collected. It enables you to check that your materials, instructions and procedures work smoothly. Let one or two people undertake the personality test to make sure they understand the questions. See how easy it is to keep a record of your own text messages too.

> *Record any problems or changes needed to your procedures/instructions here.*
>
> _____
>
> _____
>
> _____

It is a good time to try to remove as many of the possible extraneous variables as you can. If your participants complete the personality test at different times of the day, they may naturally be in different moods, which may influence their answers. Some may be hungry or tired, and not give the test their full attention. Try to ensure that they all complete the test at the same time of day.

Step 5 *Gather your data and enter all information on data sheets*

Use the psychometric test that you have chosen. Allow each participant to undertake the test you have selected in private. This will help to maintain their confidentiality. The participants must not be identifiable. A good way to deal with this is to give each person a number or code, for example, P1, P2, P3. Initials or names should be avoided. When the participant has completed the test, the total can be put in a data table like the one in step 7 on page 78.

For the second piece of information that you will gather, you must explain to the participants that they need to keep a record of how many text messages they send in one day. It would be better if you could get them all to do this on the same day, as this would reduce the situational variables. They do not need to keep a running total throughout the day as long as they do not delete any texts that they send. They can wait until the end of the specified day and count the texts then. It is important to remind them that no one wants to read their messages, you just need to know how many were sent. (Some people might not want to take part if they think you will be reading their text messages.) You can now include this second figure on your data table.

Ethical issues

When investigating people's personality, you could upset participants by drawing attention to negative characteristics. Try to provide enough information to prepare participants for this possibility before you gain their consent to participate. You could reassure the participants by telling them that the test is an indicator of how they are feeling at the time of taking the test, and they may have a different score if they take the test on a different day.

Analysing your data

Step 6 *Organise and display your data*

You should have a completed data sheet with the scores given by each of your participants. There should be two scores for each one. The first will be a number representing the total amount of text messages sent in the period they were asked to record them, and the second will be their score on the personality test. These will form the basis of your scattergram and your statistical analysis.

Step 7 *Inferential statistics and testing for significance*

In order to test for significance, psychologists carry out statistical tests to show the likelihood that the relationship/difference obtained is real (significant) rather than occurring purely by chance. Choose your statistical test using a number of types of information:

- What level of data was collected – nominal or ordinal ?
- Did the research look for a difference between sets of data or a relationship between two variables?
- If an experiment has been carried out, what type of design was used?

> **Look it up ...**
>
> You can refresh your memory about test choice using the flow chart in the Appendix on page 91.

Write down the statistical test you will use.

_____

Put your data into a table like the one below.

Participants	Number of texts sent	Rank	Score for personality trait	Rank	d	d^2
1	50	2	60	3.5	−1.5	2.25
2	75	1	34	6	−5	25.0
3	43	4	51	5	−1	1.0
4	49	3	60	3.5	−0.5	0.25
5	24	5	82	1	4	16.0
6	12	6	78	2	4	16.0

- Rank the scores of the number of text messages sent. Give the highest score a rank of 1 and the lowest score a rank of 10 (or however many participants you have). If you have tied scores, give them a tied rank (see the Appendix).
- Repeat this process for the personality test scores.
- Find the difference (d) between the rank given to the number of text messages sent and the rank given to the personality trait score, as in the table above.
- Square this difference, which will get rid of any negative scores.

- Add up the final column to calculate the total of the d^2 scores (Σd^2).
- Put your data into the formula below:

$$R_s = 1 - \frac{6\Sigma d^2}{N^3 - N}$$

Work out the formula:

- Multiply (times) the total from the last column of your table (Σd^2) by 6.
- Take the number of participants in your sample (N) and multiply this by itself to find N^2 (If you had 10 couples $10 \times 10 = 100$)
- Multiply the number of participants in your sample by the squared value minus 1 (in the case of ten couples this would be 10×99) to find $N(N^2 - 1)$
- Take your answer for $6\Sigma d^2$ and divide this figure by $N^2(N - 1)$
- Subtract the number in the previous step from 1.

You should now have a number between −1 and +1. A larger figure (closer to +1 or −1) indicates a strong relationship whereas a figure close to zero indicates a weak relationship.

- If the number is positive, this indicates a positive correlation.
- If the number is negative, this indicates a negative correlation.

> *This final number is your obtained value of Spearman's rho. Write it here.*
>
> _____

Step 8 *Interpret your results. Is the result statistically significant?*

Assess whether the relationship you have found is statistically significant or could have occurred by chance. Compare your obtained value with the critical value taken from the table in the Appendix.

- Decide where to look in the table by finding N. N relates to the number of participants used in your study.
- Check whether you had a directional or a non-directional hypothesis.
- Find the column for probability level of 0.05.
- The point in the table where these intersect is known as your critical value.
- If your result is equal to or larger than the critical value, you can reject the null hypothesis and accept the alternative hypothesis. You have found a significant correlation.
- If your result is smaller than the critical value, you must retain the null hypothesis. Your data suggest there is no relationship between the number of text messages sent by a person and his or her level of self-esteem.
- Complete the statistical conclusion on page 80.

Think about validity

Could any confounding variables have influenced the results, such as demand characteristics or untruthful answers given by the participants because they were embarrassed to give honest answers? How might this have affected the validity of your study?

*The observed value of **Rs** = _____*

This was _____ than the critical value of _____

*for **N** = _____ probability equal to 0.05*

Therefore the null hypothesis was _____

Hint

Remember that this is a correlational analysis. Whatever your conclusion might be, you cannot assume that one variable has caused the other to occur. All you can say is that there is a relationship between the two.

Critical discussion

Theory

- Did your findings support your hypothesis?
- If you retained the null hypothesis, can you think of reasons why this might be?
- Do you think this shows that the chosen personality trait is related to addictive behaviour?

Methodology

- Did you have an appropriate number of participants?
- Are you sure your participants gave honest answers to the psychometric test?
- Did the participants record their phone usage accurately?
- Were your standardised instructions clear?

Ethics

- Did your study throw up any unseen ethical issues?
- How did the participants feel about taking part?
- What have you learned about research with people?

References

Button, E.J., Loan, P., Davies, J. and Sonuga-Barke, E.J.S. (1997) Self-esteem, eating problems and psychological well-being in a cohort of schoolgirls aged 15–16: A questionnaire and interview study. *International Journal of Eating Disorders*, **21**, 39–47.

Deverensky, J.L., Hardoon, K. and Gupta, R. (2003) Empirical measures vs. perceived gambling severity among youth: Why adolescent problem gamblers fail to seek treatment. *Addictive Behaviours*, **28**(5), 933–46.

Francis, L.J. (1996) The relationship between Eysenck's personality factors and attitude towards substance use among 13–15-year-olds. *Personality and Individual Differences*, **21**(5), 633–40.

Phillips, J.G. and Butt, S. (2008) Personality and self-reported mobile phone use. *Computers in Human Behaviour*, **24**(2), 346–60.

Anomalistic psychology

11   The Barnum effect and astrology

> **Learning outcomes for this practical**
> - A1, A2, A4, A5, B1, B3, B4, C1, C3, D2, E2, E5

Hint

Check these learning outcomes against the list on page iv.

Background

Many studies have shown an acceptance phenomenon in relation to personality descriptions. This is the tendency for people to give high accuracy ratings to bogus personality feedback. This was first demonstrated by Forer (1948). Forer gave participants a personality test and told them that they would each receive a unique personality description based on the results. He asked them to rate the accuracy of the description on a scale from 0 (very poor) to 5 (excellent). In reality each participant was given the same, standard description:

> *You have a need for other people to like and admire you, and yet you tend to be critical of yourself. While you have some personality weaknesses you are generally able to compensate for them. You have considerable unused capacity that you have not turned to your advantage. Disciplined and self-controlled on the outside, you tend to be worrisome and insecure on the inside. At times you have serious doubts as to whether you have made the right decision or done the right thing. You prefer a certain amount of change and variety and become dissatisfied when hemmed in by restrictions and limitations. You also pride yourself as an independent thinker; and do not accept others' statements without satisfactory proof. But you have found it unwise to be too frank in revealing yourself to others. At times you are extroverted, affable, and sociable, while at other times you are introverted, wary, and reserved. Some of your aspirations tend to be rather unrealistic.*

Look it up ...

You may want to use your A2 Student Book to refresh you memory about the nature of self-deception and belief in exceptional experiences.

The average rating given to this statement was 4.3, which indicates a very high acceptance of this general description. Similar studies have shown that the majority of participants rate such descriptions as being either good or excellent. The acceptance of false personality descriptions has become known as the Barnum effect (after the 19th-century American showman who is reported as saying 'there's a sucker born every minute').

There has been speculation that the Barnum effect is linked to beliefs in the paranormal and an underlying tendency to be gullible. Investigations of the paranormal have failed to find any reliable evidence of paranormal phenomena, yet beliefs in such phenomena are widespread. For example, many people are convinced that the descriptions of personality traits based on birth dates from astrology are accurate. Many people read horoscopes based on astrology and are convinced that some of the predictions are correct. This practical exercise involves investigating whether there is a relationship between people's tendency to believe information they are given about themselves and their belief in astrology.

Key study

Tobacyk *et al.* (1988) Paranormal beliefs and the Barnum effect, and Standing, L. and Keays, G. (1987) Do the Barnum effect and paranormal belief involve a general gullibility factor?

Both of these studies investigated the link between the acceptance of false personality descriptions (the Barnum effect) and beliefs in paranormal phenomena. Tobacyk *et al.* (1988) hypothesised that there would be a correlation between paranormal beliefs and susceptibility to the Barnum effect. They found a strong Barnum effect with 67 per cent of their participants rating the bogus description as being good or excellent. However, there was no significant correlation to a general paranormal belief scale. There was a significant correlation between the Barnum effect and belief in spiritualism. Standing and Keays (1987) found that there was a positive correlation between the belief in the paranormal and general gullibility. However, they found no correlation between a general belief in the paranormal and the Barnum effect.

Method

Step 1 *Design your study: variables and hypotheses*

The first step of the research process is to identify a topic of interest and to choose a suitable method to investigate it. Here, the topic of interest is the relationship between participants' belief in false personality descriptions and belief in astrology. Your method is therefore a correlational study.

In a correlational study, the researcher does not manipulate an independent variable but measures two co-variables to establish whether there is a pattern or relationship between them. The two co-variables measured in this correlational study are:

- strength of belief in the generic personality description (the Barnum effect)
- the level of belief in astrology.

You will need to use a scale to measure both the level of agreement about the false personality results and the level of belief in astrology. Many such scales use 5 points between 'completely agree' and 'completely disagree'. It will help in the analysis of the results if the scales used in this study are slightly larger, so in this exercise we would like you to use a 7-point scale.

Write the hypotheses for your study. The null hypothesis states that there will be no relationship between variable *X* and *Y*, whereas the alternative hypothesis predicts a relationship. You will need to decide whether your alternative hypothesis should be directional (use a one-tailed test) or non-directional (use a two-tailed test). Non-directional hypotheses are chosen when there is insufficient research to point to the outcome of the study.

> **Think about controls**
>
> Why do all of the scales use an odd number of points between the two extremes?

Write your hypotheses here.

■ Null hypothesis _____

■ Alternative (experimental) hypothesis _____

Justify your choice of a directional or non-directional hypothesis here.

I have chosen a _____ hypothesis because _____

_____

Step 2 *Sampling*

In this study you will need to ask participants to complete a personality test on one occasion and ask them to rate the description supposedly resulting from the analysis of their answers on another occasion. So you need to select participants that you know you will be able to study on different occasions. In addition to the two study phases, there must be enough time to fully debrief the participants in this study. Remember that participants *must* be over 16. You will need to decide how to select your participants. Some possibilities include:

■ a random sample
■ an opportunity sample
■ a self-selected (volunteer) sample.

You will also have to think about sample size. You are unlikely to find a significant correlation with a small sample.

Chosen sampling method:

_____

Step 3 *Create stimulus materials, rating scales and data sheets*

This study will require the use of different stimulus materials at different stages. The first is some form of personality test. This should not be a real or standard test but one that mimics the types of question that are asked in such tests. In order for the study to work, the test must be credible. You will find many personality tests on the internet and you could use similar examples in your bogus test. A good website to look at is one that is based on the original study by Forer at http://forer. netopti.net. The test should be long enough to be credible.

Devise a question or questions about belief in astrology using a 7-point scale. The study will probably work best if this is presented on a separate sheet to the personality test as people will be less likely to think it is a trick question. If you ask more than one question about belief in astrology, you will need to calculate an average score out of 7 for analysis of the data.

> **Think about validity**
>
> Why might it be better to use more than one question about belief in astrology?

In the second phase of the study you will need a standard personality description that you can give to all participants. You could try to adapt the one used by Forer (see the background information on page 81) or you could construct your own. Forer used statements from horoscopes and these are a rich source of generic personality statements that you could use to build a general personality description. Devise a 7-point scale to measure the level of agreement with the personality description. You will need some descriptor at each end of the scale. This might ask how accurate the description was ranging from 'not accurate at all' to 'very accurate' or some other wording that shows the level of agreement.

Devise a set of standardised instructions for the participants that make it clear exactly what they need to do. Try to ensure that your instructions encourage the participants to use all of the points on the scale, not just the middle numbers.

> **Ethical issues**
>
> Remember that this is a response sheet that will have to be correlated to the level of agreement with the personality description. How can you keep the information confidential?

Step 4 *Ethical issues*

Ethical issues guide practical choices and decisions at all stages of the research process. Think about the ethical issues involved in this piece of research.

- An important principle of research is to enable participants to give their fully informed consent to take part. However, in this study you cannot do that. The Barnum effect only works if you give false feedback about personality. Therefore, although you can ask for a person's consent to take part in a study of personality and astrology, this consent will not be fully informed. You should put as much information as you can (e.g. the time commitment and the type of tasks) on to a consent form and you should present this to your participants to sign. The consent form should make it clear to your participants that they are free to withdraw at any time and that the information collected will remain confidential.

- In this study you will deceive your participants about the nature of the study. You should be aware of this throughout the procedure.

- You are asking for information about participants' beliefs and therefore you should be very careful to keep this information confidential. The data about belief in astrology and agreement with a false personality statement will be on separate sheets, but they will need to be paired up in order to correlate them. However, for ethical reasons it would be better if the response sheets were anonymous. One way of achieving this is to assign each participant with a random number, which they can put on both forms. This will link the forms while the participants remain anonymous. Once the data have been recorded into a results table, you should destroy the response sheets.

- Ensure participants are fully debriefed at the end of the study. Because deception was involved in the study, you should be very careful to explain the nature of the study and why deception was necessary. You should stress the right to withdraw from the study at this stage. This means that participants should be aware that they can quote the random number on their form and ask for their results to be removed. You should thank them, tell them what you expect to find and ask whether they have any questions. This is good ethical practice.

Step 5 *Piloting*

A pilot study is the last stage of planning, before real data are collected. It enables you to check that your materials, instructions and procedures work smoothly. Think about how and where you will collect your data. The environment you use should be kept the same (as far as is practically possible) for all of the participants. This should be relatively noise- and distraction-free.

Carry out a short pilot study testing three or four people to check that your materials and procedures work smoothly.

> *Record any problems or changes needed to your materials procedure or instructions here.*
>
> _____
>
> _____
>
> _____

Ethical issues

Did you remember to give participants a random number to identify their two response sheets?

Analysing your data

Step 6 *Organise and display your data*

You should have a completed data sheet with the scores. For each participant, you should have two scores: one for the level of agreement with the false personality description and the other for the level of belief in astrology. The scores should be put into a table like the one below and will form the basis of your scattergram and your statistical analysis.

Participants	Level of agreement with personality description	Level of belief in astrology
1		
2		
3		
4		

Plot these scores on a scattergram. Graphs provide an 'eyeball test' to give you an indication of patterns or relationships in the data. In this case, your scattergram will help you to see whether there is a relationship between the level of agreement about the false personality description and the level of belief in astrology. Remember to give your graph a title and to label both axes appropriately. Your graph could be drawn on graph paper or presented using a computer program such as Excel. On page 86 is an example of what your scattergram might look like.

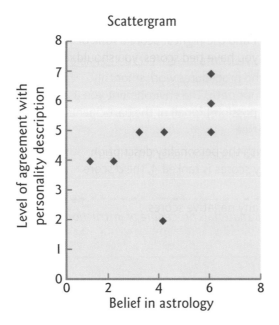

Scattergram

Describe the pattern shown by your data using the terms 'positive correlation' or 'negative correlation' and 'weak', 'moderate' or 'strong correlation'.

_____

Step 7 *Inferential statistics and testing for significance*

In order to test for significance, psychologists carry out statistical tests to show the likelihood that the relationship or difference obtained is real (significant) rather than occurring purely by chance. Choose your statistical test using a number of types of information:

■ What level of data was collected – nominal or ordinal?

■ Did the research look for a difference between sets of data or a relationship between two variables?

■ If an experiment has been carried out, what type of design was used?

Write down the statistical test you will use.

_____

Look it up …

You can refresh your memory regarding test choice by looking at the flow chart in the Appendix on page 91.

Put your data into a table like the one below.

Participants	Level of agreement with the personality description	Rank	Level of belief in astrology	Rank	d	d^2
1						
2						

- Rank the scores given to level of agreement with the personality description. Give the lowest score a rank of 1 and the highest score a rank of 10 (or however many participants you have). If you have tied scores, you should give them a tied rank (see the Appendix).
- Repeat this process for the level of belief in astrology scores.
- Find the difference (*d*) between the rank given to level of agreement with the personality description and the rank given to the level of belief in astrology score. If the level of agreement with the personality description is ranked 1 and the level of belief in astrology scores is ranked 4, the *d* score would be –3.
- Square this difference, which will get rid of any negative scores.
- Add up the final column to calculate the total of the d^2 scores (Σd^2).
- Put your data into the formula below.

$$r_s = 1 - \frac{6\Sigma d^2}{N(N^2 - 1)}$$

Work out the formula:

- Multiply (times) the total from the last column of your table (Σd^2) by 6.
- Take the number of participants in your sample (*N*) and multiply this by itself to find N^2. (If you had 10 participants, $10 \times 10 = 100$).
- Take this number minus 1 and multiply it by the number of participants in your sample (10×99) to find $N(N^2 - 1)$.
- Take your answer for $6\Sigma d^2$ and divide this figure by $N(N^2 - 1)$.
- Subtract the number from the previous step from 1.

You should now have a number between –1 and +1. A figure closer to +1 or –1 indicates a strong relationship whereas a figure close to zero indicates a weak relationship.

- If the number is positive, you have a found a positive correlation.
- If the number is negative, you have found a negative correlation.

This final number is your observed value of Spearman's rho. Write it here.

_____

Step 8 *Interpret your results. Is the result statistically significant?*

Assess whether the relationship you have found is statistically significant or could have occurred by chance. Compare your observed value with the critical value taken from the table in the Appendix.

- Decide where to look in the table by finding *N*. *N* relates to the number of participants used in your study.
- Check whether you had a directional or a non-directional hypothesis.
- Find the column for probability level of 0.05.

- The point in the table where these intersect is known as your critical value.
- If your result is equal to or larger than the critical value, you can reject the null hypothesis and accept the alternative hypothesis. You have found a significant correlation.
- If your result is smaller than the critical value, you must retain the null hypothesis. Your data suggest there is no relationship between the level of agreement about the false personality description and the level of belief in astrology.
- Complete the statistical conclusion below.

> **Think about validity**
>
> What would the results show if the participants did not believe the personality test was real?

The observed value of r_s = _____ .

This was _____ than the critical value of _____

for N = _____ probability equal to 0.05.

Therefore the null hypothesis was _____

Critical discussion

Theory

- Did your findings suggest there is a relationship between level of agreement with personality description and belief in astrology?
- If you retained the null hypothesis, why this might be?
- Did your study show a Barnum effect?

Methodology

- Were your personality test and generic description credible?
- Was your rating scale a useful way of assessing either the Barnum effect or belief in astrology? Could the method have been improved?
- Were your standardised instructions clear?

Ethics

- Did your study throw up any unseen ethical issues?
- How did your participants feel about taking part?
- What have you learned about research with people?

References

Forer, B.R. (1948) The fallacy of personal validation: A classroom demonstration of gullibility. *Journal of Abnormal and Social Psychology*, **44**, 118–23.

Standing, L. and Keays, G. (1987) Do the Barnum effect and paranormal belief involve a general gullibility factor? *Psychological Reports*, **61**, 435–38.

Tobacyk, J., Milford, G., Springer, T., and Tobacyk, Z. (1988) Paranormal beliefs and the Barnum effect. *Journal of Personality Assessment*, **52**, 737–39.

Glossary

Aggression: deliberately unfriendly behaviour that is often intended to cause harm, usually observed through verbal or physical acts.

Body dissatisfaction: feelings of unhappiness that may occur if a person's ideal body shape is very different from their actual body shape.

Carpentered environment: an environment being predominantly made up of geometrical shapes, with flat sides, straight edges and corners.

Categorical variables: a variable that is measured by counting how many people fall into one category or another.

Confidential: intended to be kept secret. Confidentiality is an important aspect of the BPS ethical principles, and results should not be disclosed or discussed outside the research.

Consent form: given to participants before they take part in research. Participants agree that they understand what is involved and how long the study will take. It should remind participants that they are free to withdraw at any time.

Content analysis: a quantitative method in which the content of books, newspapers or television programmes is examined and features are counted to see how often they occur .

Continuous variable: a variable that can produce scores of any value on a continuous scale, for example time in seconds and height in centimetres.

Critical value: the value in a statistical table that is used to decide whether the observed result is significant or not.

Debriefing: giving information to participants after they have taken part in the study, thanking them and answering any questions about the research.

Dependent variable: the variable that is affected by the independent variable.

Experimental hypothesis: a hypothesis that predicts a difference or relationship between variables in an investigation.

Hypothesis: a testable statement about the outcome of an investigation.

Independent group design: participants take part in one condition of the experiment only. Often an independent design compares two groups, one that is experimental and one that is a control group.

Independent variable: the variable that the researcher manipulates to see whether it has an effect on the dependent variable.

Inter-rater reliability: agreement between two separate raters in an observational study.

Message units: used in content analyses. These represent the visual or oral communication of a distinct element or 'statement', as decided by raters coding media such as video clips.

Moral understanding: the process by which people tell the difference between right and wrong.

Natural experiment: an experiment in which the independent variable occurs naturally and is not manipulated by the researcher.

Neuroticism: a dimension on Eysenck's personality inventory measuring anxiety.

Nominal (data): the lowest level of data, obtained when the researcher counts how many participants or observations fall into one category or another.

Null hypothesis: a hypothesis that predicts no difference or relationship between the variables. The null hypothesis is important in the statistical process as it is tested by the inferential statistical test.

Observed value: the value obtained after the statistical test is applied to the data.

Operationalise: define a variable and explain how it will be measured.

Opportunity sample: a sample of people who are easily available to the researcher.

Ordinal (data): data obtained when scores are put in order (first, second, third). Ranked data and grades are examples of ordinal data.

Participant variables: differences between participants such as age, personality and intelligence, which can affect the investigation. These are held constant in repeated measures designs and controlled by random allocation in independent designs.

Perceptual set: a bias or preparedness to see particular features of a stimulus.

Psychoticism: a dimension on Eysenck's personality inventory.

Random sample: a sample in which every member of the target population has an equal chance of being selected.

Repeated measure design: the same participants take part in every condition of the experiment. A 'before and after' study is a good example of this.

Representative: a sample that resembles the target population.

Research question: an open question often used in qualitative research that does not make a prediction.

Self-selected (volunteer) sample: a sample where the participants self select or volunteer to take part in the research.

Size constancy: the perceptual understanding that when objects are closer they look bigger (casting a larger image on the retina of the eye) but the actual object stays the same size.

Social learning theory: an influential theory proposed by Bandura in which learning takes place through observation of role models and imitation of their behaviour.

Standardised instructions: a set of written instructions informing participants exactly what they are expected to do in the study.

Statistically significant: a difference or relationship between variables, which is unlikely to have occurred by chance.

Violence: a deliberate act that is intended to cause physical harm.

Visual search: a perceptual task in which a participant scans for a particular object or feature (the target) among other objects or features (the distracters).

Decision chart for choosing a statistical test

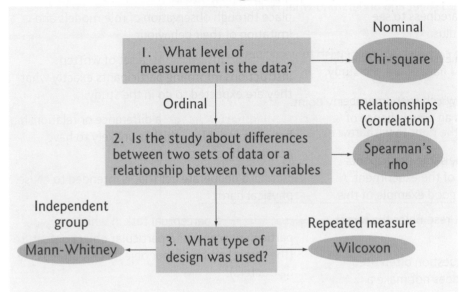

BPS Guidelines for research with human participants

At AS Level you were introduced to the BPS guidelines for research with human participants. These are listed below.

BPS guidelines for research with human participants

The British Psychological Society code of ethics, *Ethical Principles for Conducting Research with Human Participants*, covers nine different aspects of ethics that relate to research with human participants:

- Consent: participants should give informed consent.
- Deception: participants should not be misled.
- Debriefing: following the investigation the study should be discussed with participants.
- Withdrawal from investigation: participants should feel free to leave the investigation at any time.
- Confidentiality: participants have the right to confidentiality.
- Protection of participants: this includes both physical and psychological harm.
- Observational research: the privacy of participants needs to be respected.
- Giving advice: psychologists should only give advice for which they are qualified.
- Colleagues: psychologists have a duty to make sure all research is ethical, and this includes colleagues.

Check the BPS website for the most up-to-date *Ethical Principles for Conducting Research with Human Participants* (see the link to the 'Code of Conduct and Ethical Guidelines' on 'The Society' page). If you cannot remember the details from your AS studies, you should revise them now before looking at their application.

Sample consent form

> ### Consent form
>
> Please tick the box by each statement if you agree with it.
>
> I have read the information sheet and understand what I will will be asked to do. ☐
>
> I have been given time to consider whether I wish to participate and to ask any questions I have about the study. ☐
>
> I understand I have the right to withdraw at any point. ☐
>
> I understand that I have the right to withdraw my data. ☐
>
> I consent to participate in the study. ☐
>
> Signed _____

Ranking

Ranking involves giving a number to each score. This is usually done in ascending order, so the lowest score is given rank 1, the next rank 2 and so on. There should be as many ranks as there are scores. If you are ranking a set of 20 scores, there should be 20 ranks.

If two scores are the same, then they share two ranks and are given the average rank. The two participants with 12 in the example below have ranks 3 and 4 so they are both given 3.5. Note that the next-highest score, 13, is given rank 5. Similarly, if there are three identical scores, they are given the average of the three ranks they occupy. In the example, three participants have 15 and they occupy rank 6, 7 and 8 so all are assigned 7.

Table 1 *Example of ranking*

Participant	Score	Rank of score
1	15	7
2	13	5
3	18	9
4	12	3.5
5	15	7
6	11	2
7	12	3.5
8	20	10
9	10	1
10	15	7

Statistical tables

Table 1 *Critical values of χ^2*

df	Level of significance for a one-tailed test					
	0.10	0.05	0.025	0.01	0.005	0.005
	Level of significance for a two-tailed test					
	0.20	0.10	0.05	0.02	0.01	0.001
1	1.64	2.71	3.84	5.41	6.64	10.83
2	3.22	4.60	5.99	7.82	9.21	13.82
3	4.64	6.25	7.82	9.84	11.34	16.27
4	5.99	7.78	9.49	11.67	13.28	18.46
5	7.29	9.24	11.07	13.39	15.09	20.52
6	8.56	10.64	12.59	15.03	16.81	22.46
7	9.80	12.02	14.07	16.62	18.48	24.32
8	11.03	13.36	15.51	18.17	20.09	26.12
9	12.24	14.68	16.92	19.68	21.67	27.88
10	13.44	15.99	18.31	21.16	23.21	29.59
11	14.63	17.28	19.68	22.62	24.72	31.26
12	15.81	18.55	21.03	24.05	26.22	32.91
13	16.98	19.81	22.36	25.47	27.69	34.53
14	18.15	21.06	23.68	26.87	29.14	36.12
15	19.31	22.31	25.00	28.26	30.58	37.70
16	20.46	23.54	26.30	29.63	32.00	39.29
17	21.62	24.77	27.59	31.00	33.41	40.75
18	22.76	25.99	28.87	32.35	34.80	42.31
19	23.90	27.20	30.14	33.69	36.19	43.82
20	25.04	28.41	31.41	35.02	37.57	45.32
21	26.17	29.62	32.67	36.34	38.93	46.80
22	27.30	30.81	33.92	37.66	40.29	48.27
23	28.43	32.01	35.17	38.97	41.64	49.73
24	29.55	33.20	36.42	40.27	42.98	51.18
25	30.68	34.38	37.65	41.57	44.31	52.62
26	31.80	35.56	38.88	42.86	45.64	54.05
27	32.91	36.74	40.11	44.14	46.96	55.48
28	34.03	37.92	41.34	45.42	48.28	56.89
29	35.14	39.09	42.69	49.69	49.59	58.30
30	36.25	40.26	43.77	47.96	50.89	59.70
32	38.47	42.59	46.19	50.49	53.49	62.49
34	40.68	44.90	48.60	53.00	56.06	65.25
36	42.88	47.21	51.00	55.49	58.62	67.99
38	45.08	49.51	53.38	57.97	61.16	70.70
40	47.27	51.81	55.76	60.44	63.69	73.40
44	51.64	56.37	60.48	65.34	68.71	78.75
48	55.99	60.91	65.17	70.20	73.68	84.04
52	60.33	65.42	69.83	75.02	78.62	89.27
56	64.66	69.92	74.47	79.82	83.51	94.46
60	68.97	74.40	79.08	84.58	88.38	99.61

*Calculated value of χ^2 must be EQUAL TO or EXCEED the table (critical) values for significance at the level shown. Abridged from **R.A.Fisher and F. Yates** (1974) Statistical Tables for Biological, Agricultural and Medical Research, (6th edn) Longman Group UK Ltd.*

Table 2 *Critical values of U for a one-tailed test at 0.025; two-tailed test at 0.05* (Mann–Whitney)*

n_1

n_2	1	2	3	4	5	6	7	8	9	10	11	12	13	14	15	16	17	18	19	20
1	—	—	—	—	—	—	—	—	—	—	—	—	—	—	—	—	—	—	—	—
2	—	—	—	—	—	—	—	0	0	0	0	1	1	1	1	1	2	2	2	2
3	—	—	—	—	0	1	1	2	2	3	3	4	4	5	5	6	6	7	7	8
4	—	—	—	0	1	2	3	4	4	5	6	7	8	9	10	11	11	12	13	13
5	—	—	0	1	2	3	5	6	7	8	9	11	12	13	14	15	17	18	19	20
6	—	—	1	2	3	5	6	8	10	11	13	14	16	17	19	21	22	24	25	27
7	—	—	1	3	5	6	8	10	12	14	16	18	20	22	24	26	28	30	32	34
8	—	0	2	4	6	8	10	13	15	17	19	22	24	26	29	31	34	36	38	41
9	—	0	2	4	7	10	12	15	17	20	23	26	28	31	34	37	39	42	45	48
10	—	0	3	5	8	11	14	17	20	23	26	29	33	36	39	42	45	48	52	55
11	—	0	3	6	9	13	16	19	23	26	30	33	37	40	44	47	51	55	58	62
12	—	1	4	7	11	14	18	22	26	29	33	37	41	45	49	53	57	61	65	69
13	—	1	4	8	12	16	20	24	28	33	37	41	45	50	54	59	63	67	72	76
14	—	1	5	9	13	17	22	26	31	36	40	45	50	55	59	64	67	74	78	83
15	—	1	5	10	14	19	24	29	34	39	44	49	54	59	64	70	75	80	85	90
16	—	1	6	11	15	21	26	31	37	42	47	53	59	64	70	75	81	86	92	98
17	—	2	6	11	17	22	28	34	39	45	51	57	63	67	75	81	87	93	99	105
18	—	2	7	12	18	24	30	36	42	48	55	61	67	74	80	86	93	99	106	112
19	—	2	7	13	19	25	32	38	45	52	58	65	72	78	85	92	99	106	113	119
20	—	2	8	13	20	27	34	41	48	55	62	69	76	83	90	98	105	112	119	127

*Dashes in the body of the table indicate that no decision is possible at the stated level of significance.

For any n_1 and n_2 the observed value of U is significant at a given level of significance if it is EQUAL TO or LESS THAN the critical values shown.

Source: *R. Runyon and A. Haber* (1976) Fundamentals of Behavioural Statistics (3rd edn) Reading, Mass.: McGraw Hill, Inc. with kind permission of the publisher.

Table 3 *Critical values of U for a one-tailed test at 0.05; two-tailed test at 0.10* (Mann-Whitney)*

n_2 \ n_1	1	2	3	4	5	6	7	8	9	10	11	12	13	14	15	16	17	18	19	20
1	–	–	–	–	–	–	–	–	–	–	–	–	–	–	–	–	–	–	0	0
2	–	–	–	–	0	0	0	1	1	1	1	2	2	2	3	3	3	4	4	4
3	–	–	0	0	1	2	2	3	3	4	5	5	6	7	7	8	9	9	10	11
4	–	–	0	1	2	3	4	5	6	7	8	9	10	11	12	14	15	16	17	18
5	–	0	1	2	4	5	6	8	9	11	12	13	15	16	18	19	20	22	23	25
6	–	0	2	3	5	7	8	10	12	14	16	17	19	21	23	25	26	28	30	32
7	–	0	2	4	6	8	11	13	15	17	19	21	24	26	28	30	33	35	37	39
8	–	1	3	5	8	10	13	15	18	20	23	26	28	31	33	36	39	41	44	47
9	–	1	3	6	9	12	15	18	21	24	27	30	33	36	39	42	45	48	51	54
10	–	1	4	7	11	14	17	20	24	27	31	34	37	41	44	48	51	55	58	62
11	–	1	5	8	12	16	19	23	27	31	34	38	42	46	50	54	57	61	65	69
12	–	2	5	9	13	17	21	26	30	34	38	42	47	51	55	60	64	68	72	77
13	–	2	6	10	15	19	24	28	33	37	42	47	51	56	61	65	70	75	80	84
14	–	2	7	11	16	21	26	31	36	41	46	51	56	61	66	71	77	82	87	92
15	–	3	7	12	18	23	28	33	39	44	50	55	61	66	72	77	83	88	94	100
16	–	3	8	14	19	25	30	36	42	48	54	60	65	71	77	83	89	95	101	107
17	–	3	9	15	20	26	33	39	45	51	57	64	70	77	83	89	96	102	109	115
18	–	4	9	16	22	28	35	41	48	55	61	68	75	82	88	95	102	109	116	123
19	0	4	10	17	23	30	37	44	51	58	65	72	80	87	94	101	109	116	123	130
20	0	4	11	18	25	32	39	47	54	62	69	77	84	92	100	107	115	123	130	138

*Dashes in the body of the table indicate that no decision is possible at the stated level of significance.

For any n_1 and n_2, the observed value of U is significant at a given level of significance if it is EQUAL TO or LESS THAN the critical values shown.

Source: **R. Runyon and A. Haber** (1976) Fundamentals of Behavioural Statistics (3rd edn) Reading, Mass.: McGraw Hill, Inc. with kind permission of the publisher.

Table 4 *Critical values of T in the Wilcoxon signed ranks test*

	Levels of significance for a one-tailed test			
	0.05	0.025	0.01	0.001
	Levels of significance for a two-tailed test			
	0.1	0.05	0.02	0.002
Sample size				
$N = 5$	$T \leq 0$			
6	2	0		
7	3	2	0	
8	5	3	1	
9	8	5	3	
10	11	8	5	0
11	13	10	7	1
12	17	13	9	2
13	21	17	12	4
14	25	21	15	6
15	30	25	19	8
16	35	29	23	11
17	41	34	27	14
18	47	40	32	18
19	53	46	37	21
20	60	52	43	26
21	67	58	49	30
22	75	65	55	35
23	83	73	62	40
24	91	81	69	45
25	100	89	76	51
26	110	98	84	58
27	119	107	92	64
28	130	116	101	71
30	151	137	120	86
31	163	147	130	94
32	175	159	140	103
33	187	170	151	112

Calculated T must be EQUAL TO or LESS THAN the table (critical) value for significance at the level shown.
*SOURCE: Adapted from **R. Meddis**, (1975) Statistical Handbook for Non-Statisticians, London: McGraw-Hill with the kind permission of the author and publishers.*

Table 5 *Critical values of Spearman's r$_s$*

	Level of significance for a one-tailed test			
	0.05	**0.025**	**0.01**	**0.005**
	Level of significance for a two-tailed test			
	0.10	**0.05**	**0.02**	**0.01**
N = 4	1.000			
5	0.900	1.000	1.000	
6	0.829	0.886	0.943	1.000
7	0.714	0.786	0.893	0.929
8	0.643	0.738	0.833	0.881
9	0.600	0.700	0.783	0.833
10	0.564	0.648	0.745	0.794
11	0.536	0.618	0.709	0.755
12	0.503	0.587	0.671	0.727
13	0.484	0.560	0.648	0.703
14	0.464	0.538	0.622	0.675
15	0.443	0.521	0.604	0.654
16	0.429	0.503	0.582	0.635
17	0.414	0.485	0.566	0.615
18	0.401	0.472	0.550	0.600
19	0.391	0.460	0.535	0.584
20	0.380	0.447	0.520	0.570
21	0.370	0.435	0.508	0.556
22	0.361	0.425	0.496	0.544
23	0.353	0.415	0.486	0.532
24	0.344	0.406	0.476	0.521
25	0.337	0.398	0.466	0.511
26	0.331	0.390	0.457	0.501
27	0.324	0.382	0.448	0.491
28	0.317	0.375	0.440	0.483
29	0.312	0.368	0.433	0.475
30	0.306	0.362	0.425	0.467

For n > 30, the significance of r$_s$ can be tested by using the formula:

$$t = r_s \sqrt{\frac{n-2}{1-r_s^2}} \qquad df = n - 2$$

and checking the value of T in Table 3.

Calculated r$_s$ must EQUAL, or EXCEED the table (critical) value for significance at the level shown.
*SOURCE: **J.H. Zhar**, Significance testing of the Spearman Rank Correlation Coefficient, Journal of the American Statistical Association, 67, 578–80. With the kind permission of the publishers.*

Body outlines

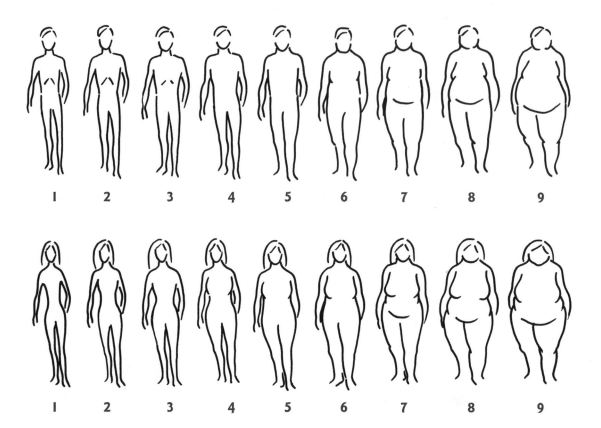

1   2   3   4   5   6   7   8   9

1   2   3   4   5   6   7   8   9